WE ARE GEELONG

The GREATEST
TEAM OF ALL

WE ARE GEELONG

The GREATEST
TEAM OF ALL

THE STORY OF GEELONG'S 2022 PREMIERSHIP SEASON

SCOTT GULLAN

Hardie Grant

BOOKS

Published in 2022 by Hardie Grant Books, an imprint of Hardie Grant Publishing

Hardie Grant Books (Melbourne)
Wurundjeri Country
Building 1, 658 Church Street
Richmond, Victoria 3121

Hardie Grant Books (London)
5th & 6th Floors
52–54 Southwark Street
London SE1 1UN

hardiegrant.com/au/books

A catalogue record for this
book is available from the
National Library of Australia

NATIONAL
LIBRARY
OF AUSTRALIA

The Greatest Team of All
ISBN 978 1 7437 9955 0

10 9 8 7 6 5 4 3 2 1

Publisher: Pam Brewster
Cover design by Luke Causby, Blue Cork
Typeset in 12/20 pt Sabon LT Std by Kirbyjones
Cover image and all images courtesy of AFL Photos
Printed in Australia by Griffin Press, an Accredited ISO AS/NZS 14001
Environmental Management System printer.

The paper this book is printed on is certified against the Forest Stewardship
Council® Standards. Griffin Press holds FSC® chain of custody certification
SGSHK-COC-005088. FSC® promotes environmentally responsible,
socially beneficial and economically viable management of the world's
forests.

Hardie Grant acknowledges the Traditional Owners of the country on which we work,
the Wurundjeri people of the Kulin nation and the Gadigal people of the Eora nation,
and recognises their continuing connection to the land, waters and culture. We pay our
respects to their Elders past, present and emerging.

'It's coming home, where it belongs!'
– Joel Selwood

CONTENTS

CHAPTER 1

PRE-SEASON

HERE he was, Chris Scott, the man who had just coached his team to an inglorious 83-point loss in the 2021 preliminary final.

For 11 years Scott had sat at the helm of the Geelong Football Club, inheriting the coach's seat at the age of 34, only a couple of years after retiring as a player, where he was feared for his ferocity whenever he pulled on the guernsey for Brisbane.

That was a very young age for a senior coach, and 11 years later a few grey flecks had crept into his beard, and sprung up around the temples, but he was just as imposing as ever.

Above all, the fire was still there, the fire that made opposition players wary whenever he was about, the fire that made him a target for opposition fans. He wasn't the grumpiest coach, or the snarliest coach, or the angriest coach – but journalists were wary of him, knowing that he did not suffer fools or foolish questions. He would answer questions thoughtfully, but also dismiss stuff that he thought was rubbish.

All 18 clubs in the AFL are playing for the one thing: the right to stand on the dais at the end of the season, holding aloft the premiership cup, being cheered by hordes of delirious fans. Lots of teams would start the season knowing they were not a chance – but would never say so in public. Lots of teams who might just be a chance to make the finals would perhaps say their aim was a premiership, hoping that might help. But among those who really do start the season with a chance of ending it with the ultimate glory, few would ever dare say so at the start of the season. It was a superstition. It was custom. It was tempting fate. It was hubris. It was just not done.

So what did Christ Scott think of the chances of his team, aged now, the oldest in the league, who had come so close so many times in recent years. Could they win it?

'Yep, I am very confident of that.'

Confidence was not something the rest of the football world had in the Cats. A big red pen had come out and drawn a line through Scott's aging team after their 83-point preliminary final loss to Melbourne five months earlier. Finally, the club that had refused to go down looked like a spent force. They were the oldest list in the competition, and for the fifth time in nine years had failed to get past the preliminary final. The one time they had jumped that hurdle, in 2020, they had blown their lead in the Grand Final, against Richmond.

While there were legitimate excuses for the poor performance against the Demons – several key members of the team had been struck down by illness, including big forward Jeremy Cameron, who lost 4 kilograms in the 48 hours before the game – the excuses fell on deaf ears.

Despite making a Grand Final the previous year against Richmond, the court of public opinion had the Cats in their sights – and in particular coach Scott. The former Brisbane Lions premiership defender had a lot of critics, which was strange given he had the best winning percentage of any coach in the competition. Actually, a better winning percentage than all the great names in coaching – Barassi, Jeans, Hafey, Malthouse, McHale, you name them.

And he was a Geelong premiership coach – only the sixth in the club's history – having come in as Mark Thompson's replacement in 2011 and guided the Cats to their third flag in five years. But that was all ancient history now, as the popular belief had his side being too old and too slow to again be a premiership contender.

They were going into the new season with 14 players either about to turn 30 or already past that milestone. In modern-day AFL, the Dad's Army approach was frowned upon.

Steve Hocking had heard all the talk but had remained at arm's length from his former club during his four years as the AFL's general manager of football. He was now returning home to fill the shoes vacated by long-time CEO Brian Cook. Hocking, who had been Thompson's right-hand man during the glory premiership years of 2007 and 2009, had already identified that Geelong had suffered more than others from the long stints away in the Covid hubs over the previous two seasons.

The whole place was tired, the players were frustrated, the coaches exhausted and the game style stale. Things had to change. Hocking set about a big reset of the club were he had played 199 games. He had some heart-to-heart conversations with Scott, made possible by the mutual respect between the pair.

The coach had also had a pivotal discussion with his team leaders, including captain Joel Selwood and co-vice-captains Patrick Dangerfield and Tom Stewart, where he asked them straight: 'Am I the man for the job again?' It wasn't so much that he had doubts about himself, it was more an understanding that after 11 years the same voice can grow stale. Coaches have a use-by date. The response he got quickly put that notion to bed.

'I made it hard for them. I said, if you have any doubt at all you have to tell me,' Scott said. 'I have done a version of that [meeting] almost every year, but at the end of '21 in particular they were emphatic and the support was the basis of my drive in 2022.'

Scott's coaching panel was overhauled, more by circumstance than design. After six years as an assistant coach focusing on defence, club legend Matthew Scarlett had grown tired – life in the Covid hubs had taken its toll on him. He resigned, while his best mate Corey Enright, having served five years as an assistant coach, went to St Kilda, knowing that he needed to test himself in another environment if he had designs in the future to be a senior coach.

Matthew Knights, the former Richmond captain and Essendon coach, had been an assistant coach at the Cats for six years. Now he was gone, a victim of the Covid soft-cap cuts that reduced coaching staffs across the game, and had headed to West Coast.

They were replaced by three-time premiership hero James Kelly, who came back to his old club after a stint as an assistant at Essendon, plus former Carlton and Adelaide great Eddie Betts joined on a part-time basis. Richmond premiership player Shaun Grigg had his role upgraded, while Scott's former Brisbane teammate and long-time assistant Nigel Lappin rounded out the new-look coaching panel. Lappin had been instrumental in the 2011 premiership.

In the AFL there is only a small window between the end of the season and the start of pre-season where change can occur. What pleasantly surprised Hocking was the person who seemed the most ready to embrace it. 'You can only achieve it through openness and the ability for people to recognise that there does need to be some shift,' Hocking explained. 'There needs to be a freshness that is brought into the place around ideas and contribution as well. Chris [Scott] has been here over 10 years now and he embraced it as much as anyone.'

In many ways it was a case of getting the old firm back together. Behind the scenes in the football department, a quiet revolution was happening, with 16 of the 34 positions changing. There was a theme to the moves: favourite sons were being brought back to the fold.

Harry Taylor returned from WA to run the club's medical services, Matthew Egan took over development, Shannon Byrnes became the runner and player development manager, while Andrew Mackie's role in the list management/recruiting department continued to evolve.

When pre-season training began, the players and staff were very aware that season 2022 was starting with a blank canvas. The game plan, which had been built on being the best defence in the competition, needed some rejigging, and this was where Scott stepped up. While some coaches have a philosophy and stick to it through thick and thin, one of Scott's strengths – which many didn't realise – was his ability to change approach based on personnel. He made it clear to his new assistants that he was all ears about what Geelong could look like in 2022.

What was clear to the newcomers was that some of the players were carrying baggage. They had come so close to climbing the mountain in recent years, only to come up short. In the 2019 preliminary final against Richmond they had been three goals up and lost. A year later in the Grand Final against Richmond they were again three goals up midway through the third quarter and lost. Then there was the memory of their most recent match: the 2021 preliminary final loss at the hands of the Demons.

The whole vibe around training was changed. Instead of over-coaching and honing in on every specific detail of the game plan, the players were given the reins to figure out their own way through new drills with a licence to make mistakes as part of their learning.

What was obvious early in the pre-season was the nucleus for a dynamic forward line was there. Cameron was fit, unhindered by injury, and did not miss a beat over the summer, which was in complete contrast to his injury-riddled first year at Geelong. Full-forward Tom Hawkins was only getting better with age, like a nice red wine. And the Cats seemed to have uncorked a special talent in Tyson Stengle, who was on his last chance at his third club – he'd been signed as a delisted free agent. He was doing things on the track that had his new teammates excited.

Moving the ball quicker into the forward line would be a priority – but to do that a collective change of mindset was required. The defenders could boast about being the best in the competition according to the stats – but now they had to think about what was happening further up the ground. What the new coaching panel was looking for was how each line could help each other – a more collective approach about ball movement and defence.

That sort of change takes time. It was going to be a slow burn, but everyone at Geelong was on the same page. There was another subtle change too: they were training themselves for the big moments in the big games at the end of the year.

Chris Scott had a spring his step again. The last time he'd felt this invigorated was his first year in the job – which happened to be the last time he and the Cats had won a flag.

CHAPTER 2

Round 1

Saturday March 19, 2.10 pm
Melbourne Cricket Ground
Geelong 20.18.138 versus Essendon 11.6.72

'HE looked like the "Danger" of a few years ago.'
Chris Scott summed it up perfectly. Patrick Dangerfield had just put on a clinic, winding back the clock with a vintage midfield performance, collecting 31 disposals, eight clearances and 12 score involvements. He was part of a first-half assault that turned the pre-season narrative on its head. Essendon had been talked up as being one of the big improvers after finishing eighth in Ben Rutten's first season as coach, while the Cats were supposedly heading in the other direction.

A seven-goal opening quarter set the tone with the lead out to 10 goals by half-time. Dangerfield was on record-breaking pace for inside 50s with nine, plus five score assists. Fellow veterans Joel Selwood (27 possessions) and Tom Hawkins (four goals) were inspired, while the good pre-season vibes about recruit Tyson Stengle were on the money as he managed four goals on debut.

But this was the Danger Show. After the awesome display, Scott pointed out the injury problems that had limited his superstar over the past couple of years. 'I don't want to go too far in my praise for him but I thought he just took the game away from the opposition early on,' Scott said. 'We've been confident in him more so than the last couple of years because he has endured some physical limitations ... our medical and sports science team have done a terrific job with him. We think there are reasons some of our more experienced players haven't quite physically been at their best and their reasons have nothing to do with age. He's been good for us the last couple of years but ... put it this way, you can't be the dominant player in the competition if you're limited physically.'

For a power athlete like Dangerfield, if anything malfunctions, no matter how small it is, the whole physical system can be thrown out of whack, which dramatically reduces output. Persistent ankle and Achilles issues had been his kryptonite in recent times, and he was even forced to make regular visits to Adelaide in 2021 to see specialist physiotherapist Steve Saunders, who'd helped him out earlier in his career. This year the Cats had hired Saunders, who'd previously worked at North Melbourne and Adelaide, as a consultant.

In many ways the 2016 Brownlow Medallist was his own worst enemy. Where others would sit out with niggles, he would still put himself out there even if he was functioning below full capacity. And for the most part a 70 per cent Dangerfield was more than good enough, still better than most. But what it did was restrict his game-breaking ability, which when in top gear was virtually unstoppable. That's why Geelong had pulled out all the stops to get the boy from Moggs Creek in 2015.

From the moment Dangerfield was drafted by the Adelaide Crows at No.10 in the 2007 National Draft, Cats fans had dreamed about the day he would come back home. He was 17 and still at school when the Crows drafted him, and he elected to stay home in his first season, playing with the Geelong Falcons and finishing Year 12 at Geelong's Oberon High School. But he did manage to sneak over for two games, kicking a goal on debut in Adelaide's Round 20 victory over Essendon.

By 2012 he was one of the best players in the competition, helping the Crows rise to a preliminary final appearance, finishing second in the best and fairest and earning his first All-Australian selection. While he enjoyed Adelaide, the pull of home was always there, and by 2014 Dangerfield decided he was going to make the move, although he was forced to keep it a secret until midway through 2015. He'd actually wanted to tell the Crows earlier and still play the year out, as happens in the NRL, but was advised by his teammate James Podsiadly, a former Cat who'd become a sounding board for him, that the AFL wasn't ready for such honesty.

Dangerfield gave everything in his final season in Adelaide, winning the best and fairest and collecting his third All-Australian jacket. In a nice twist, his last game for the Crows was against Geelong at Kardinia Park. By this stage the cat was out of the bag, as it were – and the Geelong fans cheered the Adelaide player, in the expectation that he was coming home.

And he was. In an act of good faith, Geelong worked out a trade with the Crows, which they didn't have to do given Dangerfield was a free agent who could walk for nothing. The Cats sent picks No.9 and No.28 along with young South Australian midfielder Dean Gore, who had yet to play a senior game, to Adelaide in return for Dangerfield and a third-round draft pick.

His arrival was perfectly timed. The Cats had just had their worst season under Scott, missing the finals for the first time in nine years. Dangerfield played in a memorable debut for his new club against Hawthorn in Round 1 2016, collecting 43 possessions.

A brilliant season followed, but despite Dangerfield's best efforts the Cats stumbled in the preliminary final when they froze against Sydney, allowing the Swans to kick seven goals to nil in the opening quarter. Dangerfield still found a way to have 39 touches and kick a goal, but it was a heartbreaking loss, one that would haunt Geelong and their coach for several years.

Three days later he was a Brownlow Medallist.

It was a one-sided count, with Dangerfield polling 35 votes to finish nine clear of Sydney's Luke Parker with Richmond's Dustin Martin a further vote behind. He became the third Geelong player to win the league's best and fairest award in the modern era, joining Jimmy Bartel from 2007 and Gary Ablett Jnr from 2009. The difference was they both won theirs in premiership years.

This fact drove Dangerfield even more but despite his superhuman efforts over the next few years the Cats continued to come up short. It got to the point where many believed the midfield star was almost trying too hard, convinced that he had to be the best player on the ground for his team to have any chance to succeed.

Then in his only Grand Final appearance, against Richmond in 2020, Dangerfield had one of the worst games of his career, gathering just 12 disposals and kicking one goal in the 31-point loss. By his own admission he went into a 'dark cave' afterwards. The next year, 2021, as he searched for redemption, his body let him down in another Covid-marred season.

That was a scenario the Cats' medical team were desperate to avoid in 2022. Everything was geared towards having the 32-year-old physically at his peak in September.

CHAPTER 3

Round 2

Friday March 25, 7.50 pm
Sydney Cricket Ground
Sydney 17.5.107 versus Geelong 10.17.77

IT was always going to be an asterisk game.

For six months the Sydney Swans had circled this night on the calendar as being the Lance 'Buddy' Franklin celebration.

The superstar came into the season requiring only five goals to reach the magical 1000 goals milestone, making him just the sixth player in VFL/AFL history to reach that summit, alongside Tony Lockett, Gordon Coventry, Jason Dunstall and a couple of Geelong legends, Doug Wade and Gary Ablett Snr.

In the Swans' opening round win over the GWS Giants, Franklin managed only one goal, which added to the theatre of the Round 2 clash with Geelong. Will he or won't he do it?

Ironically the first goalkicker of the night was at the complete other end of the spectrum – Jake Kolodjashnij kicked just his second goal in 134 games in the opening 90 seconds. And when Zach Tuohy followed shortly after the Cats seemed to be on a roll.

That ascendancy was short-lived as the Swans slipped into gear, kicking the next four goals, including one to Franklin. He was still stranded on that number at half-time even though his side was clearly in control, leading by 26 points after kicking four goals in a seven-minute burst. A number of Geelong prime movers had been quiet, with the previous week's hero Patrick Dangerfield having just five touches in the opening half.

When Franklin was handed a gift by the umpires midway through the third quarter after a dubious free kick against young Cat Jack Henry for falling into his back, the focus again shifted back to the superstar's quest.

A late goal in the third quarter had the security guards out circling the arena, although they were surprisingly few in number and were never going to have any hope of stopping the traditional crowd invasion to celebrate such historic moments.

With the lead out to 33 points at three-quarter time, the entire focus for the rest of the game was on Franklin getting his 1000th goal. At the six-minute mark of the last quarter Sydney's young gun Chad Warner tore through the middle of the ground and delivered a perfect pass onto the chest of Franklin on the lead. As soon as the drop punt from 30 metres left his boot, Franklin knew, as did 36,000 fans at the SCG, that it was the magical 1000th.

The crowd quickly streamed onto the ground, surrounding the Swans star while the Geelong players tried to get off the ground. It was chaos, and at one point Tuohy accidentally poleaxed a fan who dropped his wallet. The Cats defender showed his Good Samaritan side by picking it up and running back into the maul to return it.

It took security 15 minutes to get Franklin off the ground, and the game was delayed for just over 30 minutes. Some Sydney players even resorted to going out the public exits of the ground and walking around to the changerooms because it was a quicker route.

There had been an air of inevitability about the whole night from the moment the Swans showed they were committed to the contest early. Then it was the football gods joining in to ensure Sydney and Franklin had their night of celebration.

The one constant bright light throughout a disappointing Cats performance came from one of its more unassuming characters. Brad Close is a man of few words, but his football was starting to do a lot of talking. Against the Swans he was Geelong's only multiple goalkicker, with four.

Despite his low-key personality Close had started to develop a cult following, thanks in part to his love of wearing a traditional old-school long-sleeved jumper. It helped that he was now the custodian of No.45, a famous number in Cats history, having been worn for 246 games by their last premiership captain, Cameron Ling. Close received that number when he was drafted by the Cats in 2019.

Close was looking very much like another Stephen Wells special. The veteran recruiter was universally regarded as the best in the business, having more than 30 years' experience in the game. The late Geelong president Frank Costa used to joke there should be a statue of Wells out the front of Kardinia Park, given the role he played in putting together the Cats' three premiership sides.

There were so many left-field selections that had turned into gold. Corey Enright was plucked from Kimba, a dot on the map in South Australia, at pick No.47, and went on to play 332 games. Max Rooke's dad wrote a letter to every recruiter about his lad in Casterton, west Victoria, population 1500. Only Wells followed up. The rookie-lister went on to play in two premierships. Another two-time premiership player Mathew Stokes came as a mature-age recruit at No.61 while plenty of the Cats' premiership heroes came a long way down the draft, including Ling (No.38), Darren Milburn (No.48) and Paul Chapman (No.31).

Wells had never had access to anything better than No.7 in the draft, which he used twice to perfection, on Joel Selwood and Andrew Mackie, who rival recruiters scoffed at when he was taken so high given he'd only really played school footy in Adelaide. Another surprise early pick was Harry Taylor at No.17.

Wells found Close in the SANFL, where he'd just played in a premiership with Glenelg as a 20-year-old. He was originally from Mount Gambier, where as a 16-year-old he'd played in a premiership with local club North Gambier in 2014. Instead of going to boarding school in Adelaide to further his football like many others did, he elected to stay home. Another impressive season as a senior regular followed in 2015, before he tasted success again with a 35-goal season in 2016.

Operating between wing and half-forward in his customary long sleeves, Close kicked 36 goals in 2017 before making the leap to play seven SANFL games for Glenelg in 2018. The following season he played 21 matches at SANFL level, winning his third senior premiership in six years, over Port Adelaide, which was enough to catch Wells' eye.

He played eight games in his first season in the blue and white hoops and was an emergency for the 2020 Grand Final. Balancing out that disappointment was the fact he got to see first hand the great Gary Ablett Jnr in his brief return to Geelong.

'There were a lot of little tricks he taught us boys, obviously being a bit later in his career his body probably wasn't as fast or mobile as it was previously … little things like using his smarts,' Close said about Ablett. 'Little positionings, he was one of the best on the crumb and the ground balls and the way he was able to manipulate his defender and make sure he had the best positioning when the ball came to ground, little things like that I got to learn.'

In 2021 Close became a regular senior player – he played 22 games and kicked 15 goals – with his run-down tackling, pressure work and goal assists endearing him to his teammates, in particular fellow forward Jeremy Cameron. The pair struck up a close friendship when the boom recruit arrived from the GWS Giants. They bonded over their country links – Cameron had grown up just 50 kilometres away from Close in Dartmoor, in south-west Victoria – as well as a shared love of fishing and video games. The unlikely pair also quickly developed an affinity on the field, with Close regularly providing supply for his mate.

What stood out about Close was his cleanness – he didn't fumble and never lost his feet, traits that coaches love. Assistant coach James Kelly quickly became his No.1 fan: 'Every week I just fall more and more in love with Brad Close.'

CHAPTER 4

Round 3

Saturday April 2, 7.25 pm
Melbourne Cricket Ground
Geelong 16.8.104 versus Collingwood 13.13.91

COMETH the hour, cometh the man.

Geelong fans saw why their club paid the big bucks for Jeremy Cameron in an extraordinary final-quarter performance. In a game that had everything, the Cats looked gone for all money at three-quarter time after Collingwood kicked nine goals to three in the third quarter to lead by 30 points. Then 50 seconds into the last quarter Mitch Duncan kicked a goal. Mark Blicavs dobbed the next then Cameron took charge.

The former Giant, who'd already kicked three goals for the night, slammed on two in two minutes, and then his good mate Brad Close kicked another – the scores were level.

Having intelligently made space on a lead, Cameron kicked his sixth goal with 90 seconds remaining, icing the game and putting an exclamation point on his best-on-ground performance. Tom Hawkins bobbed up with his third goal for the match to give the Cats a memorable 13-point victory. Tom Stewart had also been brilliant across half-back while there were plenty of cameos in the comeback, including a couple of significant moments from young defender Sam De Koning who was thrown forward in the last quarter – including a huge handball in the chain to Cameron's sixth goal.

Fittingly it was Joel Selwood who helped spark the Cats late in what was a momentous night as he became the longest-serving skipper in the game's history, breaking the 227-game record of Carlton great Stephen Kernahan. But it was Cameron who stole the show. His match-winning performance gave the Cats a glimpse into why they'd moved heaven and earth to get him to Kardinia Park in a ground-breaking deal that almost didn't happen a couple of times.

Free agency was introduced into the AFL in 2012. This changed the game for list managers, with clubs often planning two or even three years ahead, given they know when players will become available on the open market.

Geelong had been tracking Cameron for several years for a number of reasons. At the top of the list was the go-home factor, which was a common problem for all clubs, but in particular the expansion teams, the GWS Giants and Gold Coast Suns, who lack club history and a strong supporter base, ingredients that make clubs attractive to players.

History shows there is a high percentage of draftees who want to get traded back home. The free agency period is a crossroads point – if players have any yearnings to come back, free agency is the time it becomes possible.

Cameron was a country Victoria boy from Dartmoor, population 150, known for his love of the outdoors – which automatically saw Geelong jump to the top of the list of prospective homes, given the lifestyle it can offer compared to Melbourne clubs. He had been at the Giants from day one of the club, signed as a 17-year-old in 2011 under the concessions that allowed GWS to pre-list a dozen of the best teenagers from around the country.

The 196 cm power forward was a standout junior and it didn't take long for him to prove himself in the AFL, winning the Giants' best and fairest in his second year. He kicked an impressive 62 goals for third place in the 2013 Coleman Medal and earned his first All-Australian selection despite the team winning just one game. He topped the league's goalkicking list in 2019 with 67, and was awarded his second All-Australian jumper during the Giants' march to their first Grand Final appearance, which ended badly against Richmond.

Every Victorian recruiter had 2020 marked in their diary as the year Cameron would come out of contract as a restricted free agent, which meant he could go wherever he wanted. Behind the scenes, Geelong had been on the phone to Cameron's management numerous times, asking about his plans. Midway through the season the Cats were told to cool their jets. The 'thanks but no thanks' message was delivered, with Jezza, as he is known, happy to stay at the Giants.

This was a major blow. Through a combination of good management and good timing, Geelong were in possession of a war chest of draft picks they could use in a blockbuster trade for Cameron. These had come courtesy of the West Coast Eagles and Tim Kelly. Kelly had been yet another Stephen Wells success story. The Cats took the 23-year-old electrician, unwanted in numerous drafts, at No.24 in the 2017 National Draft after he'd starred for South Fremantle in the WAFL competition.

The prolific midfielder finished second in the Sandover Medal, the league's best and fairest award. However, the two Western Australian AFL clubs snubbed him, with the Eagles and Fremantle Dockers having four picks between them before the No.24 selection.

Kelly was an instant hit at Kardinia Park, slotting straight into the senior team, playing 23 games, kicking 24 goals and averaging 22 disposals. He was rewarded with joint second place in the Carji Greeves Medal alongside Patrick Dangerfield. However, the pull of home had been a constant battle for Kelly, his partner and their three young children. He requested a trade back to WA, but when a deal couldn't be done with West Coast, it was agreed he would fulfil the second year of his contract at Geelong in 2019.

The rumour mill had Geelong asking for picks 20 and 22 in the 2018 draft and a future first-round selection from the Eagles, who baulked at the deal in a move they would come to regret 12 months later. Kelly's asking price sky-rocketed after he put together a brilliant 2019, earning All-Australian selection in a season where he averaged 25 possessions and kicked 24 goals. He was the star of the Cats' preliminary final loss to Richmond, kicking three goals from 31 disposals. As a consequence the Eagles were forced to cough up big time at the trade table to secure Kelly this time.

They offered him a six-year contract worth an estimated $800,000 per season, which was almost four times what he'd earnt a season at Geelong. To get the deal done the Eagles handed over two first-round picks – No.14 in the 2019 draft and a future first-round selection in 2020 – plus selections No.24 and No.33. In return they received Kelly, pick 57 and a future third-round pick.

It was one of the biggest deals of its kind, but Wells wasn't finished weaving his magic. In a stroke of genius he sent selection No.24 to the Gold Coast for the Suns' 2020 mid first-round priority pick. The Cats went on to use pick No.14 (pushed back to No.16) at the 2019 NAB AFL Draft to secure local midfielder Cooper Stephens, before using their own No.19 on a tall defender by the name of Sam De Koning.

As exciting as that was, the deal meant that in 2020 – the year that Cameron was coming out of contract – Geelong had a mouth-watering three first-round picks at its disposal. While they had all the right bait to land the big fish, Cameron wasn't biting until a phone call in Grand Final week.

As the Cats were preparing to play Richmond in their first Grand Final since 2011, Cameron's manager informed the club that his man was reconsidering his future and open to pulling on the hoops. Life in the Covid hubs had really affected Cameron, who had hated being holed up in hotel rooms all year as the competition was forced to relocate to Queensland because of the pandemic.

On the field he'd had a poor year (24 goals from 17 games) and off it he'd had plenty of time to weigh up his life. Change was what he wanted, and while the Giants tried a last-ditch bid to win him over with a fancy lunch at one of Sydney's leading restaurants with assistant coach Steve Johnson, coincidentally a former Cat, and chief executive Dave Matthews, their persuasive powers weren't enough.

Cameron had become stressed out and barely slept, he said, in the two months before his decision. 'There were so many nights when I went to sleep thinking, "I want to make the move" and then I'd wake up and I wanted to be a Giant. That's how intense it was for me,' Cameron said.

Intense was exactly how you'd describe the negotiations between the two clubs. As a free agent Cameron could choose a new home, but there was a curveball, as under the rules of free agency the Giants were allowed to match any offer from the Cats. This had never happened before. The Giants wanted to keep their man. They matched the Cats offer, which was estimated to be around $4.5 million over five years.

The move surprised the Cats as it now meant the only way Cameron would get to Geelong was through a trade – and GWS wanted some serious compensation for one of the game's best forwards.

Enter the Tim Kelly picks.

The Cats offered two of the three picks they'd received for Kelly (15 and 18), plus their own first pick (25). In the end they knew Cameron was the type of talent who could be the difference between winning a premiership or not. He was worth the price. However, as part of the deal, Geelong wanted two second-rounders back. And this is where things got messy.

The deal came down to the final two minutes of the 10-day trade period, with the Cats considering whether they attempted the risky play of walking Cameron through the draft. Geelong chief executive Brian Cook, who had swapped emails with the Giants in the taxing lead-up, was blunt about the frantic final few minutes. 'It was messy, really messy,' Cook said. 'There were some renegotiations in the last 90 seconds around the deal. It was a really tight, tough and challenging last two minutes to say the least.'

There was even a suggestion the paperwork hadn't been finalised until after the deadline as both clubs wrangled with technology, but it eventually got the tick of approval from the AFL with Geelong getting their two future second-round picks (one tied to GWS, the other to Essendon in 2021).

The deal evoked memories of the last time Wells had gone big at the trade table for Richmond ruckman Brad Ottens, dealing picks No.12 and 16 back in 2004. That worked out pretty well, with the big man helping the Cats to three flags.

Commentator David King was thinking the Cameron trade could do something similar after watching the final-quarter burst against Collingwood. 'When they got rolling, this is as good a football as you'll see,' King, the former North Melbourne premiership star, told Fox Footy. 'It was the most powerful of quarters I've seen in a long time. And this guy [Cameron] finished with six goals, including three in a hurry in the last quarter.

'I just feel like with Jeremy Cameron's acquisition, you're buying wins and it's going to be there for a long period of time. They're incredibly dangerous now with those two forwards [referencing Tom Hawkins]. They are just a wildcard. Most of us have said, "Can they get it done?" But not many teams can play like that.'

CHAPTER 5

Round 4

Friday April 8, 7.50 pm
GMHBA Stadium
Geelong 11.14.80 versus Brisbane 11.4.70

JOEL Selwood was to be rested in Round 4.

While the captain had been involved in plenty of discussions with Chris Scott, assistant coach Shaun Grigg, Harry Taylor and his conditioning team about how they were going to handle his workload this year, when the crunch came in Round 4 it was still a hard pill to swallow.

Telling a warrior like Selwood to sit out a game is no easy task, but the conversation was had in the lead-up to the Friday night blockbuster against Brisbane. Selwood knew it was for the greater good and that's what Geelong was about this season. Everything was focused on the end of the season – getting their inspirational skipper to September fit and firing was the priority.

It also set a good example for the rest of the team, reinforcing the message that the big picture was the priority – and if that big picture cost a win or two here and there, then Scott and the coaching team could live with that.

Life without Selwood was bad enough, then just an hour before the game All-Australian defender Tom Stewart and Esava Ratugolea were withdrawals, making things a whole lot harder. Stewart, the reigning Carji Greeves medallist, was stripped to play but was pale as a ghost after having been hit with a severe bout of gastro, and was consequently ruled out by the doctors.

It was a far from ideal scenario, particularly given the Cats were aware Brisbane were coming to town fizzed up for the contest. An intense and at times bitter rivalry had grown between the two sides, with the tensions boiling over in the corresponding game the previous year. An off-the-ball hit by Gary Rohan on Brownlow Medallist Lachie Neale had stirred up proceedings early, with spice added when Scott got into a verbal altercation with Lions players at the quarter-time break. Selwood and Cam Guthrie had had to intervene and steer their coach back to the huddle, but that wasn't the end of the fireworks.

Once the huddle broke up and Scott was heading off the ground up to the coaches' box, there had been an exchange with Brisbane coach Chris Fagan. Then to add to the drama the game was decided by a missed free kick against Cats defender Mark Blicavs, which would have handed Lions forward Zac Bailey the chance to kick the match-winning goal from 5 metres out. Geelong had hung on to win by one point. The AFL's later ruling that the umpiring decision to not penalise Blicavs for incorrect disposal was a mistake just rubbed salt into the Brisbane wound.

There were differing versions from both camps after the game about who said what in the fiery quarter-time exchanges. 'I wouldn't choose to speak to opposition players,' was Fagan's take afterwards.

Scott said he reacted to a barb from Neale, who was clearly frustrated as he'd been tagged out of the game by Irishman Mark O'Connor. 'I was walking onto the ground and Lachie Neale just said to me something like – I couldn't understand exactly what he said – but something about Gary Rohan,' Scott said. 'And I said, "I'm happy to have the conversation with you if you like. I've seen the vision and I'm comfortable with it." I suspect he didn't hear all of that. That's all that was said. I think a few of them weren't paying me compliments. I didn't say anything after that.'

The upshot was clear: these two teams didn't like each other – and that was front and centre in the lead-up to the 2022 clash.

Fagan was also trying to break a few of his team's interstate hoodoos. They hadn't won at the MCG since 2014, losing 11 straight. Their record at GMHBA Stadium was no better, not having tasted victory at the Cats' home ground since 2003. As it happens, Scott had played in that Lions victory, alongside his twin brother Brad. That was during the Brisbane glory days, when they were an invincible force, beating up on young teams like Geelong during their dominant era of three consecutive premierships from 2001 to 2003.

One famous story from those encounters involved Lions captain Michael Voss who, during a game against the Cats at Kardinia Park, called the umpire to stop play early in the third quarter. "Stop the game! Stop the game!' Voss said before pointing to young Cats rover Shannon Byrnes. 'I think one of the Auskickers has been left on the field!'

The Scott boys were known as 'The Kray Brothers', feared figures in London's criminal underworld of the 1950s and 60s. On the football field the twins had a fierce aggression and fearless intent that intimidated opponents. Their renowned toughness sometimes took away from the fact that both were very talented footballers. Chris won the Rising Star Award in his first season, 1994. He went on to play in two premierships during his 215-game career, which ended prematurely because of injury in 2007.

How he ended up at Geelong as a senior coach three years later is courtesy of a couple of significant sliding door moments.

First there was an AFL intervention that ensured Scott, who started his coaching apprenticeship at Fremantle immediately after he retired, came to the attention of Geelong powerbrokers Steve Hocking and Neil Balme. As part of the game's 150th birthday celebrations, the AFL staged a Hall of Fame Tribute match between Victoria and a Dream Team in 2008. Reigning premiership coach Mark Thompson was the Vics' coach. He wanted his trusted Geelong lieutenants –assistant Brenton Sanderson and footy bosses Balme and Hocking – to oversee the team. The AFL were happy with that but had one provision: Thompson had to include one assistant coach from another club.

Enter AFL administrator Rod Austin, who nominated Fremantle's first-year assistant. Scott was Thompson's conduit on the bench in the exhibition match that night. He impressed the Geelong hierarchy, who came away convinced he was a senior AFL coach in the making.

Fast forward to late 2010 and the Geelong empire appeared to be crumbling. A horror preliminary final thrashing at the hands of eventual premier Collingwood was followed by the exit of their best player, Gary Ablett Jnr, to the Gold Coast. And then Thompson, who'd been at Geelong since 2000, shocked the football world by quitting and moving back to his old club Essendon to help its new coach, James Hird.

While this was happening Scott had made the decision to throw his hat into the ring for the vacant Port Adelaide coaching job. The Power were looking for a replacement for premiership coach Mark Williams midway through the season. After going through the interview process, Scott narrowly missed out on the job to caretaker Matthew Primus.

Scott would later say that the experience made him ready for when Geelong came knocking. If he hadn't done it, he believes he wouldn't have got the Cats job. 'I was going through it, to be brutally honest, for the experience because I had no idea how to go about it or what was involved,' Scott said. 'I was really raw. I wouldn't have got the Geelong job if I didn't go through the process at Port.'

While two of Geelong's favourite sons – 11-year player Sanderson and another former Thompson lieutenant Ken Hinkley, a Carji Greeves medallist – were considered the favourites to take over from Thompson, Balme and Hocking recommended to CEO Brian Cook that Scott should also be interviewed.

Geelong's criteria included an emphasis on the coach having been part of a successful environment, that he be under 40 and a premiership leader. Scott ticked all the boxes, and this time being a favourite son did not help – there was a consensus among the Geelong hierarchy that an outsider was preferred. A month after missing out on the Port job, the 34-year-old won the Cats' role.

Within 12 months he was a premiership coach. Port had done him a favour by overlooking, and ended up dispatching Primus within two years.

And so here Scott was 11 years later, facing up to his old team, who were going to be in the premiership race, which added extra fuel to the Round 4 clash.

Of the new rivalry with the Lions, Scott said: 'The way I see the rivalry and I've always been of this view even when I played back in the dark ages – it is a privilege to be part of a rivalry because they are really rivalries when you get two contenders. When you're playing the best teams, it has more of an impact than every other game because it is a competition. You're not just trying to win your game, but you are trying to take one away from the other, so that always adds a bit more spice to the genuine rivalries.'

Fagan, who took the top job at Brisbane in 2017, described the match-up as an 'intense rivalry'. 'Geelong have been up there a long time and they like to stamp their authority on other teams that might be emerging,' Fagan said. 'Hopefully we can show them we're really maturing as a team.'

This game helped entrench the rivalry. Geelong's mature players held firm in a tight contest, which saw the home team trailing by one point going into the final quarter. Three goals to one in the last quarter was enough to get the job done for the Cats, with Tom Hawkins' fifth goal the sealer. Fellow veteran Isaac Smith was best on ground in the 10-point victory, with 29 disposals. His hard running and penetrating left boot netted him an impressive 623 metres gained. Some flashes of brilliance from Sam De Koning caught the eye.

Mitch Duncan was particularly damaging in the first half with 14 touches, which included four score involvements. He switched from the midfield to half-back to play Stewart's quarterback role, doing so brilliantly – the luxury of being able to use him as a defender added another dimension to the Cats' new game plan.

A plan that was slowly starting to take shape.

CHAPTER 6

Round 5

Monday April 18, 3.20 pm
Melbourne Cricket Ground
Hawthorn 14.8.92 versus Geelong 11.14.80

IT had become one of the more enjoyable days on the AFL calendar.

Easter Monday at the MCG between arch rivals Geelong and Hawthorn rarely failed to deliver. In 11 editions of the public holiday match-up, the Cats had won nine times, with the margin in single figures five times.

The first game back in 2010 set the tone for the next decade with a grandstand finish between two sides who were then at the peak of their powers. There was some Buddy Franklin brilliance and Steve Johnson magic before the Cats finally edged in front with five minutes to go after a courageous mark from Paul Chapman. A Shannon Byrnes rundown tackle and goal then sealed the nine-point win. Gary Ablett Jnr had risen to the occasion with 38 disposals, Brad Ottens earned the three Brownlow votes and Cam Mooney booted four goals.

Two years later and it was Geelong's wet weather specialist, Jimmy Bartel, who put on a clinic to drag the Cats back into the match for a memorable two-point victory. Hawthorn had led by three goals going into the final quarter before Bartel took over. When James Podsiadly roved the ball that had gone over the back of the pack in the goal square, the Cats were in front with six minutes remaining. The Hawks had a chance to win the game with 15 seconds on the clock when Jack Gunston crumbed the ball off the pack, but his quick snap trickled to the wrong side of the post to hand Geelong a thrilling two-point victory.

It was a similar tale in the opening round of the 2013 season when captain Joel Selwood led a second-half comeback, taking the Cats from three goals down to 21 points up midway through the final quarter. But as is seemingly always the case in these Easter Monday clashes, there was another chapter to be played out, as the Hawks responded with two quick goals before some Cyril Rioli magic set up Luke Breust for a chance to further cut the margin with 90 seconds remaining. From 30 metres out on a slight angle Breust shanked the set shot, ending hopes of a miracle comeback. The seven-point victory kept the infamous Kennett curse going, making it 10 consecutive wins for the Cats against Hawthorn since the underdog Hawks beat them in the 2008 Grand Final. It was then that the Hawthorn president and former Victorian premier had boasted: 'What they don't have, I think, is the quality of some of our players; they don't have the psychological drive we have.'

Hawthorn broke Geelong's winning run in the opening round of 2015 with a 62-point smashing. Their only other victory came in yet another epic in 2018, which this time had the Cats flying home late. The Hawks led by four goals with 12 minutes remaining before the Cats rallied with a snap by Brandan Parfitt levelling the scores with just four minutes left on the clock. In the end it was some moves by veteran Jarryd Roughead to outbody young Geelong defender Zach Guthrie for the game-winning mark. While he missed the set shot, a behind was enough to seal a famous victory.

The Easter Monday fixture was back in 2021 – Covid had nixed it in 2020 – and it served up another close one, which got decidedly uncomfortable for the Cats after they'd led by 30 points late in the third quarter. Hawthorn proceeded to kick six of the next eight goals to get within a kick before running out of time. The Cats got home thanks to a Jordan Clark intercept at centre half-back, which saw him run the length of the ground and receive a handball to kick the winning goal. Hawk fans booed Isaac Smith all day as he played his first game against his old club. Smith, as ever, just smiled. Cam Guthrie knocked up 43 disposals, in what was arguably the best game of his career.

It was fertile ground for Geelong, the Easter Monday fixture, and it was expected to continue in 2022, with the experienced Cats coming up against a very young Hawks outfit, who were going through a generational change and all the pain that comes with it, under the guidance of new coach Sam Mitchell.

Hawthorn, however, clearly hadn't read the script.

The Hawks caught the Cats napping. Emerging star Jai Newcombe dominated the middle of the ground, goal sneak Dylan Moore kicked three goals in the opening term, and the Hawks raced to a 23-point lead at the first break. Finally the Cats woke from their slumber with Hawkins, Jeremy Cameron and Tyson Stengle kicking three goals each to earn a 12-point advantage at three-quarter time.

For most of the 48,000 present, the game was done, Geelong poised to roll through for a regulation victory after an early scare. But once again Mitchell's men weren't ready to accept someone else's script. Instead they kicked four goals to none in the final quarter, full-forward Mitch Lewis kicking the sealer from the goal square with two minutes remaining to send Hawks fans wild.

It was a miserable day for the Cats on a number of fronts. Jack Henry was subbed out as a precaution after feeling pain in the same foot he had surgery on in the off-season. And again Patrick Dangerfield was the focus of questions for Chris Scott post-match after having only 17 disposals, just three of them in the last quarter when the game was on the line.

The Cats' coach confirmed he continued to manage some ongoing issues. 'He's had a few little niggles that haven't kept him out of games that might be holding him back a little bit,' Scott said. 'He wouldn't like to use that as an excuse ... he's been in really good shape through the pre-season. I think he's going to have a better year this year than he has the previous two.'

On his long drive back down the Geelong Road to Moggs Creek that night, Dangerfield wasn't as optimistic as his coach. He was frustrated. The surgery he'd had on a syndesmosis tear in his right ankle the previous year, which saw him miss six games, had aggravated his Achilles heel, which was now causing issues with his calf.

And it was giving him a disturbing sense of deja vu.

CHAPTER 7

Round 6

Sunday April 24, 1.10 pm
Blundstone Arena
Geelong 17.19.121 versus North Melbourne 9.7.61

OR Zach Tuohy it had become an obsession.

The clock was ticking and he knew it. Every day his mind would wander to the thought of holding up the AFL Premiership Cup. He was already a driven person – you don't move to Australia from Ireland to play a sport you'd barely heard of if you're not made out of something special – but this year it had gone to another level.

Tuohy was 32 and in the final year of his contract. He'd played finals every year since he joined the Cats in a trade from Carlton at the end of 2016. A Grand Final loss and three preliminary final defeats had cut deep. The disappointment would actually cause him sleepless nights as he lay in bed staring at the ceiling wondering: 'Have I just blown it?'

'The focus of my AFL dream has always been about winning a premiership,' Tuohy said. 'It's why I came to Australia and it's become much more of a focus during the back half of my career. The last few years though I've been slightly obsessive about winning a flag, particularly because I'm closer to the end of my career than the start.'

A hamstring injury had struck late in the 2021 season, which threw everything out, although he did get back for the semi-final and then more disappointment in *that* preliminary final against Melbourne. 'That kills me much more than it used to,' he said.

With that at the forefront of his mind, Tuohy didn't miss a beat over summer. He was physically the best he'd been in years and was a man on a mission, something history showed he was pretty good at completing.

It had all started with a phone call back in 2008.

Gerard Sholly, a recruiter for Carlton, had tracked down the Tuohy family's phone number because he'd liked what he'd seen of the teenager playing Gaelic football for his county Laois. Zach was the youngest of four boys. His father, Noel, was a warder at the Portlaoise maximum security prison.

AFL was well and truly on the radar in Ireland. Only a few years before Tadhg Kennelly's exploits at Sydney, where he played in the Swans 2005 premiership side, had made headlines. The great Jim Stynes, Brownlow medallist and all-round inspiration, was a big man. Colm Begley, who grew up 10 minutes down the road from Tuohy, was also making a fist of it in Brisbane. Tuohy knew there were scouts out from Australia watching games.

Sholly wanted to know if he was interested in coming over for a four-week trial at Carlton. Tuohy jumped at the opportunity. He did enough to get an invite back, and in 2010 he settled in Melbourne to pursue a new life.

He was assigned to the Blues VFL affiliate, the Northern Bullants, and after his first few games he was by his own admission 'a million miles away from playing AFL'. But while the structures and dynamics of the game were challenging, what Tuohy had was toughness, commitment and a booming right-foot kick. Luckily he also had another Irishman, Setanta Ó hAilpín, at the Blues who helped him get over regular bouts of homesickness.

With the help of development coach David Teague – who would go on to coach the Blues years later – Tuohy improved quickly to the point where Carlton drafted him at selection No.73 in the 2010 Rookie Draft. He made his debut the following year in Round 11 against Port Adelaide, sitting on the bench for three quarters as the substitute.

An impressive long goal the following week in his second game had people taking notice. He held his place in the side for several weeks, lost it, then was a late inclusion into the semi-final side, which lost narrowly to West Coast.

He soon became a regular in defence for the Blues. By 2015 he had improved to the point of finishing third in the club best and fairest. Brendon Bolton arrived as coach for 2016, which was another disappointing season for the club, never threatening to play finals. Tuohy decided he needed a change of environment.

'Towards the end of 2016, I felt like my time at Carlton was almost up,' Tuohy, who hadn't missed a game since the start of the 2013 season, said. 'With the path they were going down, I don't know if many people there saw me as part of the future at the club. That was based on just gut feel and also the contract they put in front of me.'

The Cats swooped and sent former first-round pick Billie Smedts to Carlton along with a future first-round pick and pick No.63 in the 2016 draft. They received Tuohy and a future second-round pick in return. He fitted straight in and has evolved his game in recent years, spending more time up around the midfield, where his elite kicking has become a weapon for the Cats.

The full Tuohy kit was on display against North Melbourne in Hobart as he hoovered up everything across half-back, collecting 32 possessions – the second-most of his career – as the Cats were never threatened by the struggling Roos. It was party time up forward with the big three combining for 13 of Geelong's 17 goals. Jeremy Cameron was unstoppable with seven goals, Tom Hawkins kicked four and Tyson Stengle two.

'Jeremy has been with us for a year and a half but he's missed a lot of footy too,' Geelong coach Chris Scott said after the match. 'He's going to have outstanding individual games. What we're after is that cohesion in that group … we saw some good signs of that.'

Another highlight was teenage debutant Ollie Dempsey who had his own bare-chested cheer squad in Hobart. The 19-year-old, who was the No.15 selection in the 2021 Rookie Draft, kicked a goal early in the third quarter, which saw his former schoolmates in the outer lose their mind. 'He was exciting for us. He did some things that we'd seen at VFL level and that's rarely the case in a debutant game. It's such a jump from VFL footy, even when you play in a solid win, it can be a little daunting. But I didn't think he showed any signs of that.'

CHAPTER 8

Round 7

IT was like rubbing salt into every Geelong fan's wounds.

The sight of Jordan Clark dashing down the wing at GMHBA Stadium in a Fremantle jumper to set up another Dockers surge was not the ideal scenario that afternoon for the home side. In many ways Clark had become the poster boy for disgruntled Cats fans, who'd been bemoaning the lack of pace and urgency in Chris Scott's game plan.

The No.15 selection from the 2018 draft was quick, he had the leg speed Geelong was craving, yet he'd never nailed down a spot in his three years at the club. A dashing half-back flanker was the role that he'd been pencilled in for, but, for a variety of reasons, in particular issues around the defensive side of his game, he'd never made the position his.

After 32 games, Clark requested a return home to Western Australia. A deal was done with Fremantle involving the Cats receiving draft pick No.24 and a future 2022 third-round selection.

It was rare for Geelong to have players wanting to leave and they'd now lost two WA players in two years – Tim Kelly and Clark. Drafting players from interstate had long been a subject for debate among recruiters, because of the inevitable go-home factor.

There was no doubt however that the Cats looked local first. The line-up this day against Fremantle boasted six players who'd played for the Geelong Falcons in the Victorian statewide U/18 competition – Tom Stewart, Tom Atkins, Jed Bews, Luke Dahlhaus, Shaun Higgins and Gryan Miers. Dahlhaus and Higgins had returned to their home town after stints at the Western Bulldogs and North Melbourne respectively. Stewart and Atkins were mature-aged recruits via the local league and the Cats VFL program, with Bews a father-son selection. Miers was picked by the Cats at No.57 in the 2017 National Draft, while Bews was picked up six years earlier under the father-son rule, his father, Andrew, having played 200-plus games for the Cats.

But that wasn't it for the Falcons mafia – there were another eight players on the list who'd spent time in the program, which had been run brilliantly for decades by former Geelong great Michael Turner.

These included three senior regulars who were currently out injured – Patrick Dangerfield, Gary Rohan and Jack Henry. There was also another father-son selection, Sam Simpson, 2019 first-round pick Cooper Stephens, Mitch Knevitt, Cooper Whyte and ruckman Toby Conway, who'd been selected with the pick gained from the Clark trade.

Fremantle came to town with a 5-1 record in a surprisingly strong start to the season, although they arrived without three key players: Brownlow Medallist Nat Fyfe, ruckman Sean Darcy and full-forward Matt Taberner. Geelong would have been feeling confident, especially as the Dockers had won only three times from 18 attempts at Kardinia Park.

Three quick goals to start the game, two of them from Tom Hawkins, would only have boosted that confidence. At the quarter-time break the Cats had five straight on the board to lead by nine points.

Chris Scott had warned there would be some teething problems with the new game plan, and he was on the money. The Dockers' pressure saw the Cats fall back into bad habits, moving the ball slowly, which dried up the scoring dramatically. They had lost the run of Max Holmes, who had quickly become an important cog thanks to his speed on the wing, when he was substituted early in the second quarter with an ankle injury.

The Dockers got out to a 23-point lead early in the final term before Geelong launched one of its typical late comebacks, with goals to Dahlhaus and ruckman Rhys Stanley making things interesting. Speedster Michael Frederick got one back for Fremantle at the 20-minute mark, which Tyson Stengle answered a couple of minutes later. Mark Blicavs then kicked his second goal for the day from long range, cutting the margin to three points with 26 seconds left on the clock.

Any chance of a miracle victory was snuffed out by Dockers veteran David Mundy who made sure he got his hands on the ball at the next centre bounce, preventing a Geelong clearance and killing off the game.

Once again Stewart had been the Cats' best, tallying a career-high 40 disposals including 13 marks, while Cam Guthrie continued to build into the season with 35 possessions and eight clearances.

Scott was philosophical afterwards, which again gave an insight into his big-picture thinking in 2022. 'It's frustrating now but … it's not the end of the world for us,' he said. 'I think we've shown patches where we've looked as good as the best teams. Melbourne are the best team but there's a big pack chasing.

'It's just going to be a struggle throughout the year, so the challenge is to not throw in the towel and let the bad days snowball into consecutive bad days. But also not to get too high on your toes when you do have some good patches. We have just got to keep it level, keep fighting, keep working on our game.'

That's exactly the attitude that met the players when they arrived at the club for the Monday review of the Fremantle loss. The focus was on the good patches of play in the first and last quarters, where they moved the ball the way they'd been training to do it over the pre-season.

Those were the edits being shown at the video review. The messaging was all positivity and encouragement. The players needed to believe in what they were creating. Scott and his coaches already had the sense that when their game clicked properly, it was going to be spectacular.

CHAPTER 9

Round 8

Saturday May 7, 4.35 pm
Manuka Oval
Geelong 12.16.88 versus GWS Giants 4.11.35

THE game has never seen anyone like him. And it probably won't again.

Mark Blicavs is a talent that comes along once in a generation, an athlete-turned-footballer-turned-superstar who for a decade has defied logic in every way. And for those who'd become complacent about appreciating his gifts, Blicavs decided to send an all-points bulletin to the competition via the GWS Giants in the nation's capital.

An hour before the bounce of the Round 8 encounter word got out that Geelong ruckman Rhys Stanley was a late withdrawal because of an ankle injury. So who did Chris Scott replace him with? A half-back flanker. There was no need for a like-for-like scenario because Geelong has Blicavs.

At 198 cm Blicavs has literally played every position on the ground. Full-back, centre half-back, wing, centre, ruck-rover, ruck, half-forward, forward pocket: at some stage he's been there during what is an extraordinary 200-plus-game career.

Against the Giants, Blicavs was re-programmed as the No.1 ruckman. This season he'd been mainly utilised around the midfield in different guises and also as a back-up for Stanley. Don't forget, he did win a best and fairest as a key defender.

The Giants tag teamed him with 206 cm Braydon Preuss and 201 cm Matt Flynn, both big, old-school ruckmen. They won the hit-outs 49 to 25, yet Blicavs emerged as best on ground, an architect of the Cats' emphatic 53-point victory.

Blicavs played essentially an extra midfielder, gathering 26 disposals which included 11 contested, eight clearances and six inside 50s. He also had 21 hit-outs, eight tackles – extraordinary for a tall man – and five intercepts, with the Cats only losing the clearances by one, 33 to 34, despite what on paper should have been a clear advantage to the home side.

For the past decade Blicavs has been getting a lot right after Cats recruiting manager Stephen Wells decided to take a punt on the kid from Sunbury who hadn't even picked up a football for six years when he was recruited.

As the Geelong Football Club tell it, this incredible story started back in 2001 when Andrew Guthrie, former Essendon and Fitzroy player and father of current Cats Cameron and Zach, was coaching the Sunbury Lions Under 11s, a club located about 40 kilometres north-west of Melbourne.

Blicavs was his star player, finishing equal second in the league best and fairest (behind a kid named Mitch Banner, who would go on to be drafted by Port Adelaide). His parents, Andris and Karen, both represented Australia in basketball, while his sister Sara followed suit, becoming an accomplished WNBL player and also representing her country. But it wasn't basketball or football that Blicavs pursued; rather a career in athletics, where he was one of the state's best junior steeplechasers.

Years later Guthrie was at a lunch for parents of new players at Geelong, after his oldest boy had been drafted by the Cats in the 2010 National Draft, when he struck up a conversation with Wells. Wells had heard Blicavs' running career wasn't going according to plan, and Guthrie told Wells he should reach out to the now 20-year-old, recalling that as a junior he 'had a big leap and could seriously play football'.

In early September 2011, Blicavs accepted an invitation to meet with Geelong at the MCG, where they were playing Hawthorn in the qualifying final. A secret trial was organised and Wells saw enough to read out Blicavs' name at No.54 in December's Rookie Draft. But before he fully committed to football, Blicavs asked if he could make one last-ditch attempt to make the 2012 London Olympics, not in the steeplechase but on the track in the 1500 metres.

Luckily for Geelong, he didn't make the cut, and in July 2012 he played his first competitive game of football since he was 14, pulling on the jumper in the Cats reserves side.

Remarkably, he blossomed so quickly that when a spate of injuries hit the club's tall stocks over the summer Blicavs was selected to play in the 2013 season-opener against Hawthorn on Easter Monday.

'I've never seen a 198 cm runner like him,' Scott said at the time. He didn't look out of place, having eight disposals (one kick, seven handballs) and 11 hit-outs in Geelong's seven-point win.

Blicavs was used predominantly as a ruckman in his first season, playing 22 games, including the Cats' three finals. He began to move around as his knowledge increased over the next couple of seasons, playing in the midfield and on the wing, but it was his work as the second-man-up in ruck contests that became his calling card.

This dominance around the ground and in the air in 2015 saw him win the Carji Greeves Medal after just 66 games, only three years after taking up competitive senior football.

Blicavs was elevated to the leadership group in 2016, but his world changed dramatically at the end of that season when the AFL made the abrupt decision to not allow players to jump third-man-up at ruck contests.

It took away his major weapon and his career drifted for a little while before Scott re-programmed him as a full-back to great effect. Blicavs won his second Carji Greeves in 2018, which prompted a lucrative five-year contract extension. Scott regularly describes Blicavs as 'one of the great football stories' and still marvels at the weapon he has at his disposal – as did the Giants on this day.

Jeremy Cameron lifted for the occasion against his old team, kicking three goals in the opening term. He finished with five as the Cats overwhelmed the Giants, who could manage only a miserable four goals for the night.

Two more debutants were unveiled, with Cooper Stephens coming in for captain Joel Selwood, who missed with a minor quad strain. Mitch Knevitt started as the medical sub and got his chance when defender Jed Bews was knocked out in the second term.

Patrick Dangerfield had 28 disposals in his return while Stanley's replacement, Zach Guthrie, had no trouble slotting in, racking up 23 touches, 12 marks and a goal.

'It speaks to the system that the people at Geelong have built over a long period of time, that Zach Guthrie can come in and play the way he did. If you're not being developed well, it's hard to come in and play like that,' Scott said.

CHAPTER 10

Round 9

Saturday May 14, 4.35 pm

Marvel Stadium

St Kilda 13.12.90 versus Geelong 11.14.80

I t was the greatest player rivalry of the modern era: Wayne Carey versus Glen Jakovich.

One of the game's most dominant centre half-forwards in history was pitted against the chiselled man mountain out of the west, who refused to yield to anyone. Carey, the brash young captain of the Kangaroos, humiliated defenders for fun throughout the 90s – but not Jakovich, the no-nonsense powerhouse of the dominant West Coast backline.

The Eagles were the team of the early 90s, collecting flags in 1992 and 1994. The Kangaroos hit their straps shortly thereafter, with Carey elevating them to the best team of the second half of the decade, their flags coming in 1996 and 1999. Between them Carey and Jakovich played in six grand finals and collected four premierships. Their match-ups became much-anticipated viewing, captivating the football world. The pair traded blows 17 times from 1992 to 2001, and there was no clear winner across that time.

The two players were often playing a game within a game. As long-time Eagles chief executive Trevor Nisbett saw it, 'The strange thing was that, if Wayne got on top of Glen, the Kangaroos didn't necessarily win the game. Wayne kicked five goals a couple of times on Glen, but they [North] didn't win. If Glen blanketed Carey, we didn't necessarily win the game.'

Football craves such rivalries, as much as it does team rivalries, like the one Geelong was establishing with Brisbane. This was why Chris Scott was referencing a rivalry between two up-and-coming 21-year-olds, who look destined to be playing on each other for as many years as Carey and Jakovich did: Geelong's Sam De Koning and St Kilda's Max King.

The pairing had been talked up in the lead-up to the Round 9 clash – and it certainly delivered.

King was already an established gun and was playing his 47th game, while De Koning had come out of nowhere – he'd only played one game before the start of the 2022 season – to now be the Cats' No.1 tall defender.

'He's [De Koning's] been a real positive for us,' Scott said, with a touch of the usual coach's understatement, balancing that with an acknowledgement of King: 'He's probably the best young key forward in the comp, Max King.'

And like the Carey-Jakovich match-up, the judges were ruling a draw after King kicked two goals and De Koning had 15 touches and plenty of good moments in their 10-point defeat at the hands of the Saints.

De Koning was destined to play football. His older brother by 18 months, Tom, plays in the ruck for Carlton, and they're part of a family of 10 kids, led by mother Jackie and father Terry, a one-time Footscray ruckman. They hail from down on the Mornington Peninsula, at Safety Beach, although have always holidayed over the other side, on the Bellarine Peninsula at Torquay, where the boys honed their love of surfing, and where the family was slowly but surely drifting to.

Terry De Koning is a long-time PE teacher at St Bede's Mentone, while Jackie is a performing arts teacher at Rye Primary School. Seven of their 10 children now live in Torquay, where Sam is building a house on a block that backs onto a sister's place. Meanwhile, he and another brother are renting a house Tom owns nearby.

Sam spent a lot of time following his big brother around, starting at Auskick when he was three years old. Family legend has it that when he was asked what he wanted to be when he grew up, he replied: 'Better than Tom.'

After playing juniors at Mt Martha and then the Dandenong Stingrays in the U/18 NAB League, Tom was drafted by the Blues at No.30 in the 2017 National Draft. He made his debut the following year but didn't cement a regular spot until midway through 2021.

Sam put his name up in lights when he was selected at full-back in the All-Australian team at the 2019 U/18 national championships. On draft night there were some raised eyebrows about the discrepancy between Sandringham Dragons' Fischer McAsey, who was named at centre half-back in the All-Australian team, going at No.6 and De Koning slipping through to the Cats at No.19.

Geelong was pleasantly surprised and while their new key defender didn't play a game in his first year, they couldn't have been happier with the way he developed, training alongside two-time premiership defender Harry Taylor in his final season.

It was an invaluable experience with De Koning cracking it for one game in 2021 where he kicked two behinds from eight touches against North Melbourne in Round 5. He then had to bide his time again before a spot opened up in defence following the retirement of Lachie Henderson.

In Round 1 2022 he matched it with Essendon's giant Peter Wright and hadn't looked back since, his non-fussed attitude impressing his teammates.

'First of all it's hard enough to find someone who can take the ball so cleanly below their knees at 195 cm let alone when they're 204 cm in their third year of footy,' Patrick Dangerfield said.

'He takes on all the big monsters and still takes his marks. The thing that impressed me the most about DK is he would miss a kick or get a goal kicked on him and he just doesn't care. He's like "OK, whatever", it doesn't stop him from going for his marks and that is such a strength.'

While De Koning's battle with King had excited Scott, not much else about the game did. The Cats' coach uncharacteristically delivered a bake to his team at three-quarter time. The third quarter had been a train wreck as St Kilda ran riot, kicking five goals in a 10-minute burst off the back of ruck dominance by Paddy Ryder and Rowan Marshall. A seventh goal for the term by Saints forward Tim Membrey on the three-quarter time siren gave them a 16-point advantage after they'd trailed by 22 points soon after the main break.

The Scott spray worked, for a moment at least, with two quick goals by Tom Hawkins getting the Cats within three points, before Ryder completed a stellar night by kicking two goals of his own to ensure his team's victory.

Again it had been a patchy performance with flashes of brilliance followed by sub-standard efforts, particularly around the middle of the ground where the contested ball numbers flatlined. And that's how Geelong's premiership hopes looked: pretty flat. They were in seventh place with a 5-4 record.

Something had to change.

CHAPTER 11

Round 10

IT started out as a regulation session shooting the breeze between Shaun Grigg, Nigel Lappin and James Kelly.

The three assistant coaches were preparing for the weekly match committee meeting where anything goes – no matter how crazy or left-field the idea, they're encouraged to be thrown up for consideration around the table.

'What about Axe?'

The words hung in the air for a moment and they both looked at each other. They were discussing the need for more consistent pressure around the ball, because it had been too erratic in its execution through the first half of the season. It had cost them the game the previous week against St Kilda. This was one of the things that had to change. There were reasons for the inconsistency: leaders Joel Selwood and Patrick Dangerfield had been coming in and out of the side, and speedster Max Holmes had also been sidelined. All the problems around the contest had been laid bare in the third quarter the previous week against St Kilda – when the Saints flicked the switch, the contested ball count plummeted with the Cats minus 14.

The 'Axe' they were referring to was Tom Atkins. He'd played most of the past 18 months as a lockdown defender. He was as hard as they come – he powered around the field in his 180 cm frame and could sure hit hard. When he first broke into the AFL side in 2019 it was as a pressure forward, so he ticked a few of the right boxes, but was now in defence. A check of his GPS numbers suggested that he had the running power required to be around the ball.

The one area in which the Cats had a surplus was defenders, so sending one on assignment elsewhere wasn't going to rock the boat.

'We went through the running metrics from the previous six weeks and his were the same as the midfielders', Kelly explained. 'Then we were like, "What is the worst thing that can happen?" He just comes back down and plays back again. The other by-product of it was that it would keep Zach Guthrie in the team as well.'

Chris Scott was on board, so, at the opening bounce of the Round 10 game against Port Adelaide, Atkins strode into the centre square and planted himself next to reigning Brownlow Medallist Ollie Wines.

As far as challenges go they don't get much bigger, but Atkins had made a habit of overcoming them on his long and winding road to the big time.

After not going through the traditional TAC Cup pathway, he was playing for Geelong College when Paul Hood, the Cats VFL coach, invited him to pre-season training. 'In Year 12 I was playing footy and I was never a chance for that draft, so it's not like I was like other kids where they had a bit of interest in their 18-year-old year,' Atkins recalled. 'I was just playing footy and then when Paul Hood asked if I wanted to train with the VFL I thought I would because I wanted to play as high as I could.'

And so started a special relationship.

Atkins began on the VFL's development list in 2014 and played five games; the following year he made the main list but still only played six games. In 2016 he played a full season and won the best-and-fairest award. By this stage he'd seen his teammate Tom Ruggles progress from the VFL to the AFL list, which for the first time planted the seed of a similar progression in his own mind.

'It [AFL] was never really a reality for me coming through,' he said. 'But 2017 was probably the year where for the first time I thought I was a chance. I thought if I have a really good year here, maybe Geelong will be keen on me, but then I got injured.'

A dodgy hamstring kept him sidelined for a couple of months, and while he played well at the end of the season, the Cats decided to go with Stewart Crameri with their only pick in the Rookie Draft. It hurt, but not for long, and not too deeply.

'Again, it was so far from what I thought was actually possible, so it was never like I really got my hopes up. Mum and Dad will tell you as well, I told them the whole way through that I'm going to expect the worst and then if the worst happens then I won't be let down. I was never shitty or anything.'

This attitude is what endeared Atkins to Geelong officials. Football boss Simon Lloyd was still impressed long after the fact by a text exchange between the pair when he told him that he'd missed out again.

'I understand putting a list together is a tricky job and not everyone can be a winner,' Atkins texted. 'Bigger things going on in the world mate I still get to have a run around in the twos! Will catch you round the club.' The way he handled it, the dignity, the willingness to cop it on the chin and keep going, is still used as an example for anyone who now steps into the football club.

And Atkins' response? He won his second best-and-fairest in 2018 as captain, was named in the VFL Team of the Season and produced double-digit tackles in 10 of his 20 VFL games. Given forward pressure was the new direction for the Cats, the call he'd been waiting for finally arrived with confirmation his name was to be called out as Geelong's first pick in the Rookie Draft.

The 23-year-old had been setting up life as an accountant after completing a commerce degree at Deakin University. His lifestyle wasn't one of an AFL player – he lived with three mates and takeaway was certainly at the top of the dinner list. In the lead-up to his debut in Round 1 of 2019, Atkins let slip that he'd been forced to change his diet and give away his favourite, fish souvlaki, which gained a lot of traction in the media, particularly after it was highlighted on Channel 7's popular footy comedy show, *The Front Bar*.

Having the spotlight on him wasn't Atkins' style and three-and-a-half years later that attitude hadn't changed, as he was about to become Geelong's game-changer in his 67th game. After a tight first half in which the visitors had their noses in front, the Cats took the torch to the Power in the third term and proceeded to kick seven of the last eight goals of the game to emerge comfortable 35-point winners.

The clear highlight was once again delivered by Jeremy Cameron, producing another moment of jaw-dropping brilliance. With just seconds remaining in the third quarter, the key forward brought down a colossal contested mark on the 50-metre arc. Then as the siren sounded he unleashed an epic 55-metre torpedo, sailing through for an unforgettable goal that sparked wild scenes in the stands.

Cameron finished with three goals, as did Tyson Stengle, while Cam Guthrie was again the Cats' best, recording a game-high 37 disposals, including 15 contested possessions and 12 score involvements. He polled the three Brownlow Medal votes, but in the AFL Coaches' Association Player of the Year Award there was a spread of seven players who received recognition from Scott and Port's coach Ken Hinkley. Atkins was one of them for his 19 disposals, five tackles and four clearances. For Kelly and Grigg it was a vote of confidence and confirmation they just might have stumbled across something special.

CHAPTER 12

Round 11

Saturday May 28, 1.45 pm

GMHBA Stadium

Geelong 15.7.97 versus Adelaide 7.13.55

'I THINK he's the best defender in the game.'

Chris Scott's declaration about his vice-captain Tom Stewart came after he'd watched him seemingly bring his own Sherrin against the hapless Adelaide Crows. Every time the Crows tried to go forward, the ball inevitably ended in the hands of the No.44, who had a career-best stats line of 40 disposals, 16 marks, 17 intercepts and a stunning 874 metres gained.

Scott couldn't help but let his mind wander back to the previous year's final series, which Stewart had missed because of a foot injury.

'Tom Stewart was just sensational today. If we didn't have him behind the ball when they were winning the stoppages it would've been really difficult for us,' the Cats' coach said. 'He's improving, that's probably the best description, off a very, very high base. He's important for us. He was crucial for us last year. To lose him going into the finals was a big loss and I think we're seeing exactly what a loss that was right at the moment.'

It would have been an even bigger loss if fate hadn't intervened and cleared a path for Stewart to find his way to the AFL.

In his own words Stewart was a 'fat chippy' when he was playing for local Geelong Football League side South Barwon. He played in two premierships with the Swans. Importantly, the second one in 2013 was alongside recently retired Geelong great Matthew Scarlett. Scarlett was a club legend at South Barwon, having played juniors there. He had popped his head in at club functions from time to time, but Stewart had been too shy to introduce himself.

'My first ever memory [of Scarlett] was in pre-season when we were doing one-on-one drills and I stepped up and he smashed me about four or five times in a row,' Stewart recalled.

'I kept going back and trying and that may have shown him I was a competitor and wanted to have a go. It wasn't so much a kick in the bum, it was that he saw something in me that I didn't see in myself at that stage.'

Stewart had been a part of the Geelong Falcons system but by his draft age he was in and out of the side so ditched it to play with his mates at South Barwon, where his life unfolded as it did for so many young men.

He started a carpentry apprenticeship, worked from 7.30 am to 4.30 pm, trained a couple of nights a week, played on Saturdays with beers on Saturday night. But Scarlett saw something in the attacking full-back, who by this stage was playing interleague, and encouraged him to re-evaluate his life.

'I was living with my mates in a shared house, living that life and enjoying footy, but I thought I was wasting my time,' he said. 'I looked at myself and said, "Do you want to be remembered as a local footy legend or someone who tried at the next level?"'

He was asked by the Geelong talent manager at the time, Troy Selwood to play VFL in 2016. He thrived to the point where recruiter Stephen Wells wanted him to stop playing for fear other clubs would grab the local lad with the tattoos and headband.

Luckily for the Cats, they didn't. Geelong selected the 23-year-old at No.40 in the 2016 National Draft. Despite a shoulder reconstruction keeping him off the track until Christmas, Stewart made a quick impression and was told he was debuting in Round 1 against Fremantle by his coach ... Matthew Scarlett.

The game was over in Perth at Subiaco Oval with the new Cat quickly finding himself matched up against Brownlow Medallist Nat Fyfe, universally acknowledged as one of the best players in the land.

'I took a mark on him and nudged him out and I was like, "This is nuts,"' Stewart recalled. 'I remember it vividly.'

With Scarlett and fellow Cats legend Corey Enright – whose old number he wore – on the coaching panel, Stewart flourished in the professional environment, and in his second season earned All-Australian selection before he'd even played 50 games.

In 2019 he was third in the best-and-fairest and All-Australian again. He won the club's Carji Greeves Medal in 2021 despite missing five games, then the best interceptor in the game also earned his third All-Australian team-of-the-year selection.

And now he was doing what Scarlett did with him back in South Barwon: mentoring a younger protégé who had the world at his feet.

Sam De Koning was fast emerging as a contender for the NAB Rising Star and he earned a nomination off the back of 19 disposals, nine marks and 11 intercepts against the Crows.

'I'm trying to keep the lid on it a little bit [with De Koning],' Scott said after the 42-point victory. 'I don't know how long ago it was … but he played a game and our supporters here at Geelong were going, "We love this guy right now but we're going to love him a lot for the next 10 years."

'A couple of weeks ago I thought he had a great contest [against Max King]. I likened it to Glen Jakovich and Wayne Carey, that might be a little bit of an exaggeration as they're two of the greats, but I think Sam has the potential to be one of those guys that people go to the footy to see.'

The usual suspects got the job done for the Cats – who were helped by Adelaide's inaccuracy in front of goal – with Cameron Guthrie (34 disposals), Joel Selwood (24 disposals and 13 tackles) and Brandan Parfitt (30 disposals) prolific.

Gryan Miers capitalised on his opportunities with three goals while Jeremy Cameron bagged four. Another first-gamer was introduced, 203-cm athletic forward Shannon Neale, while Tom Atkins further embraced his new role with a career-high 17 tackles. His seamless transition into the midfield helped mask the concerns behind closed doors about the man he was replacing, injured superstar Patrick Dangerfield, who the club had decided to put on ice.

Dangerfield had been subbed out a week earlier after getting another knock on the calf. The decision was made to rest him for at least three weeks until after the bye round – the Cats were sticking to their guns, keeping their eyes on the prize, the Grand Final, and wearing the pain through the home-and-away games.

Scott said it was necessary to take short-term pain in order to try and avoid what had happened in the past two years.

'Taking a bit of short-term pain to have him in the best shape possible at the end of the year, that may well cost us along the way,' he said. 'But in my opinion that is a better approach for us to take with him. We think this is going to have him in the best shape to have a really good run at the last couple of months of the season.'

He revealed Dangerfield hadn't been able to train since the start of the season but had convinced the coaches and medical staff that he was still able to play.

'A big portion of the issue right at the moment with Pat is that almost from the first round, he hasn't been able to train much,' Scott said. 'He has just had a series of issues that have stopped him training without necessarily stopping him from playing. And we have just come to that point now where we're not going to take the risk that if we just keep muddling along, he is going to be less than his best.'

The Cats' coach said Dangerfield 'might be the most explosive player of his generation' but was currently lacking his renowned power.

'That lack of explosiveness that we're seeing is down to a series of really significant corks that probably should have kept him out for a couple of games where he convinced us he can get through. So now we have put a line in the sand and said "we're not going to accept that you can just get through, we want you to play when you can get back to your best".'

Sitting sixth on the ladder at 7-4, the Cats weren't yet at *their* best – but they were picking up speed.

CHAPTER 13

Round 12

Friday June 3, 7.50 pm
Marvel Stadium
Geelong 12.11.83 versus Western Bulldogs 10.10.70

FOR Mitch Duncan it had been on the agenda for some time, but the timing had never been right.

Injuries at the wrong time in pre-season hadn't helped. But circumstances had changed and the penny had dropped for Duncan and the Geelong coaching staff – it was time to embrace life as a half-back.

Although it did come with a caveat.

The team's best user of the ball had been handed a licence to roam, given his chief responsibility was to create offence. Remember, the job of the defence line had been refocused, redefined: it was to make life easier for the forwards, to get the ball to them more quickly and more accurately.

Duncan, a second-round selection in the 2009 draft, was a student of the game, so once the move became permanent in Round 8 he started spending more and more hours in James Kelly's office learning the art of his new role.

'It had been in the pipeline probably a couple of times throughout the last couple of years,' Duncan said. 'I was probably just injured at the wrong time of the year, in the pre-season, and you need to learn the craft so we haven't been able to do it.

'The move came about because we were getting stuck with our ball movement a little bit in the early periods of the season and I just get down there and try and create. I obviously wasn't down there to defend. But I have had to slowly try and work on my defensive craft which I've actually found really refreshing – learning a different side of the game has been great for me.'

Duncan played in the 2011 premiership side, starting in the substitutes' vest before getting on for the second half after an injury to forward James Podsiadly. Since then he'd grown into one of the Cats' most important assets, who strangely will most likely finish his career without any major individual accolades.

He's never won a best and fairest – his best was finishing second behind Patrick Dangerfield in 2017 – or been rewarded with All-Australian selection, despite being around the edge of the squad a number of times. That didn't do justice to what his silky right boot had done for this team – just ask Tom Hawkins – and his reputation as a big-game performer.

And once again it was Duncan the Cats turned to in their time of need during their Round 12 clash with fellow premiership contender the Western Bulldogs. There had been no issues early in the contest with Duncan joining in the goal fest, kicking his team's seventh goal of the first quarter. It was blistering football and a snapshot of how they'd been wanting to play since the first day of pre-season.

Once again Jeremy Cameron was the centrepiece, kicking three goals from 10 touches, including the 500th of his career, as the rampant Cats shot out to a 40-point lead early in the second quarter. However, the whole complexion of the game changed when Tom Stewart was concussed after a clash with Bulldogs young gun Bailey Smith when he ran in open-chested to intercept a mark and copped an accidental knock to the jaw.

With Stewart subbed out, Duncan's importance at half-back tripled, although he had a lot on his plate as the resurgent Dogs hit back. By half-time the margin had been reduced to four goals, which had been whittled down further to a mere 11 points at three-quarter time. Geelong had ground to a halt, registering just two behinds in the third quarter.

Tensions boiled over shortly after the three-quarter time siren with Smith reported for headbutting Zach Tuohy (he would later cop a two-week suspension).

A Tom Hawkins goal in the first 50 seconds of the last quarter stopped the rot, but five minutes later the Dogs were within five points after two quick goals.

Enter Cameron.

Once again Geelong fans got to see why their club had invested so heavily in the player who was now in the conversation as being the best in the competition, kicking three last-quarter goals, including two in two minutes in time-on to snuff out the Dogs.

It was a win full of merit given the Cats were down on troops, particularly in the defence, with Jake Kolodjashnij a late withdrawal due to health and safety protocols. Stewart was off the field and still coming to his senses, which meant forward Gary Rohan had to make a rare venture down back, along with Irishman Mark O'Connor.

Duncan did his thing with 29 disposals to find himself in the votes – but once again the post-match discussion was all about Cameron. His six-goal haul took him to the top of the leaderboard in the Coleman Medal race on 38 goals, which was just one less goal than he'd kicked from 15 games in his injury-interrupted first season at the Cats in 2021.

Jeremy Cameron kicking goals for Geelong in Round 12.

Hawkins' two goals against the Dogs saw him move to third on 33. The much-hyped two-pronged forward set-up was clearly starting to gel. More importantly, recent history showed it was the premiership model.

Richmond had Jack Riewoldt and Tom Lynch together for two of their three flags, West Coast's one-two punch of Josh Kennedy and Jack Darling delivered a premiership in 2018, while the best of the modern era was Buddy Franklin and Jarryd Roughead, who were unstoppable in the Hawks' golden run. In 2008 Franklin kicked 113 goals – which was the last time the century was passed – while Roughead chimed in with 75.

While those numbers will most likely never be seen again, the Cameron-Hawkins combination, with a more than handy contribution from Tyson Stengle, who'd kicked 23 goals in the opening 12 games, had the rest of the competition on edge.

Cameron's breathtaking skill and agility for his size had most shaking their heads, but it was his trademark around-the-body set shots for goal that continued to leave his coach gobsmacked.

'When he first arrived … it wasn't even the full-blown training, it was just the mucking around with the ball pre-training that made my eyes pop out of my head,' Chris Scott recalled. 'If I was standing the mark 49 metres out on the boundary and the guy with the ball turned his body to kick a snap, I would have laughed at him. But no-one laughs at Jez.'

The win put Geelong fourth on the ladder – the first time they had been in the top four since after the opening round. The upcoming bye in Round 13 would be a well earned break for the resurgent Cats.

CHAPTER 14

Round 14

Saturday June 18, 4.35 pm

Optus Stadium

Geelong 12.9.81 versus West Coast Eagles 9.9.63

T HE big moment came from a weak free kick.

Cooper Stephens bombed the ball long from the half-forward flank onto the head of Tom Hawkins, who couldn't quite stick the mark. The ball fell to ground, and opponent Jake Waterman found himself in an awkward position – and laid an even more awkward tackle front-on around Hawkins' neck. The tackle posed no danger to Hawkins, barely impeding him, but it was a free every day of the week. The umpire duly blew his whistle, and Hank went back, turned, and snapped an easy goal around the body. It was his 700th goal.

It seemed like destiny for Hawkins, who had come to the club as a mere boy.

Hawkins grew up on a farm in Finley, in country New South Wales, pretending to be Gary Ablett Snr, with the No.5 on his back. He was a diehard Cats fan from day one, but he probably had no choice, because his father Jack had played 182 games in the blue and white hoops. He was a prodigious talent, nicknamed 'Jumpin' Jack' for his frequent spectacular high marks.

'Certainly Gary Ablett senior was my childhood idol,' Hawkins said about reaching the 700-goal milestone. 'I am 34 next month and I have been at the footy club for 16 years, which is just about half of my life. I came to the footy club as a boy and I have grown as a man in the last 16 years and it has been a wonderful journey.

'Gary Ablett senior was my favourite player growing up and I obviously knew about Doug Wade through family and older generations that have told me about him. It has been pretty cool to sit alongside those guys and obviously the footy club has a rich history with success so it is nice to be alongside them. I have a few more to go to catch up to them but it is cool.'

Hawkins was referencing the two Geelong goalkicking legends who preceded him.

Wade is arguably in his sights on 834 goals, if you count only his goals for the Cats (but another 223 for North Melbourne has him perched on 1057, which might be a bridge too far). Likewise Gary Ablett Snr, another member

THE GREATEST TEAM OF ALL

of the magical 1000-goal club, with 1031 goals to his name (which includes 10 kicked in his first season, when he played six games with Hawthorn).

'I was lucky enough to watch Buddy Franklin kick a thousand and I thought that was one of the best things I've ever seen in footy,' Hawkins said, referencing the Round 2 match earlier in the year. 'I've got 300 to go! It's a nice milestone and I've got my dad and my brother [Charlie] over here, it's nice.'

The Hawk loves kicking goals – but he loves giving them away too. His presence at the pointy end of the goal-assists honour board tells a deeper, hidden story. He clearly enjoys his teammates kicking goals as much as he enjoys kicking them himself.

Coming into the milestone game against the Eagles, Hawkins was third on the list with 260 assists, needing only one to equal his premiership teammate Gary Ablett Jnr. Eddie Betts, the former Adelaide and Carlton star who was now on the Cats coaching panel, had set up the most goals for others, totalling 318.

There is one particular goal assist that stands out, from Round 3 2019.

He was deep forward when Jordan Clark, in just his second game, slipped in front of Melbourne's Nathan Jones and took the mark. Sensing his opportunity, the youngster saw an open forward line and ran into it, bouncing the

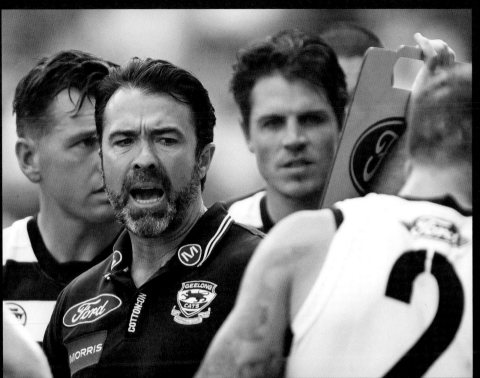

ROUND 1: WIN
Coach Chris Scott addressing the team at half-time in the season's first match, against Essendon. At half-time Geelong were on track, leading 12.9 to the Bombers' 3.3. Geelong, thought to be on the way down, trounced Essendon, who were thought to be on the way up.

ROUND 2: LOSS
Paddy Dangerfield made a beeline for Buddy Franklin at the end of the match to congratulate him on kicking his 1000th goal. As soon as Buddy kicked the goal, thousands of fans poured onto the Sydney Cricket Ground to celebrate, making it impossible for the players to reach out to him.

ROUND 3: WIN

RIGHT: Jeremy 'Jezza' Cameron kicked six goals against Collingwood, his sixth with only 90 seconds left on the clock.

BELOW: Joel Selwood receives a guard of honour for captaining the most games in AFL/VFL history – 227.

ROUND 4: WIN
Isaac Smith kicks the ball in a close match against the Brisbane Lions, when at the last change the difference was only one point. It was a sign of who Geelong would have to beat later in the competition

ROUND 5: LOSS
Tyson Stengle celebrates a goal in the match against Hawthorn, but despite Tom Hawkins, Jeremy Cameron and Tyson Stengle kicking three goals apiece, Hawthorn came out the winner on Easter Monday.

ROUND 6: WIN

A weekend down in Hobart for Geelong and North Melbourne resulted in another early win for Geelong with Zach Tuohy stepping up for the Cats.

ROUND 7: LOSS

Rhys Stanley competes with Brandon Walker of the Dockers for the ball at GMHBA Stadium in a close game. Fremantle got away from the Cats who lost by only three points, a rare loss at home.

ROUND 8: WIN
A determined kick from Mark Blicavs as Tim Taranto of the Giants tries to tackle him in the match between the Greater Western Sydney Giants at Manuka Oval.

ROUND 9: LOSS
Sam De Koning gets a handball away as St Kilda's Cooper Sharman tries to bring him down. After a strong start, the match was a disappointing loss for Geelong, but they had no idea at the time that it would be their last.

ROUND 10: WIN
Tom 'Axe' Atkins gets the ball away in an important match against Port Adelaide, and the beginning of their winning streak to the finals.

ROUND 11: WIN
Tom Stewart marking the ball in the Sir Doug Nicholls Round, as Adelaide were overrun by the surging Cats, who won by 42 points.

ROUND 12: WIN
Leading 44 to 11 at the end of the first quarter, Geelong couldn't be blamed for feeling they were well placed for a win – but the Western Bulldogs fought back. By the end of the match Geelong won by only 13 points. Cameron Guthrie played hard for what was a key win against a tough team.

ROUND 14: WIN
After the bye, Tom Hawkins was firing as he kicked this goal – a massive achievement – it was his 700th goal. Geelong went on to win by 18 points against West Coast in Perth.

ROUND 15: WIN

Tom Stewart and Dustin Martin wrestle for the ball in a ferocious match at the MCG against Richmond that saw every ounce of energy expended to win by just three points at the siren. The match was a turning point for Geelong who moved from fourth place to second place on the ladder.

ROUND 16: WIN

Following the close call with Richmond this round turned out to be Geelong's biggest win of the season with Geelong winning by 112 points against North Melbourne. Rhys Stanley played his part with this tap-out in the ruck.

ball, drawing an opponent to him, then executing an easy handball over his head to Hawkins, all by himself in the goal square. Normally the matter would end there, with an easy goal to the full-forward. Which was about to happen – until he saw the bigger picture. Instead of sending the Sherrin into the second level of the stand, Hawkins turned back towards Clark and beckoned him in, handballing the ball to the youngster so he could kick the first goal of his career. In the coaches' box Chris Scott just laughed.

Another key point about the 2020 Coleman Medallist, who has led Geelong's goal-kicking for the past 10 seasons, is that he has actually got better with age. Since turning 30, he has kicked 228 goals from 89 games, at an average of 2.4 a game. Overall, he has 724 goals from 324 – at an average of 2.2 a game.

His close friend Joel Selwood, who walked into Geelong on the same day as Hawkins after the 2006 National Draft, said Hawkins isn't defined by his goals. 'He's been sensational for the footy club,' Selwood said. 'He's just been playing awesome footy throughout the last couple of years, and to reach 700 is just touching the edges on what he does for the footy club.'

What he did for his footy club against the Eagles was save them from a whole world of embarrassment.

In 2022 West Coast had been a shadow of their former selves, never recovering after their Round 2 loss to North

Melbourne, when a raft of players were struck down by Covid and its associated protocols. Coach Adam Simpson had to field players he had never even met before. So here they were, sitting last on the ladder with just one win, which meant there was minimal expectation about anything other than Geelong chalking up its fourth straight win. But the Eagles were clearly buoyed by the return of premiership stars Elliot Yeo, Willie Rioli and Dom Sheed, and they hit the lead early in the third quarter.

Fittingly, Hawkins' third goal of the game sealed the 18-point victory. Tyson Stengle continued to hit the scoreboard with three goals, while Mark Blicavs and Rhys Stanley dominated the ruck, and Selwood (24 disposals) and Cam Guthrie (25 disposals and 13 tackles, a quarter of his team's tally) were prominent.

There was a significant inclusion for the Cats with Sam Menegola, who had knee surgery in the off-season, looking good with 20 disposals and two goals in his first game of the year.

Afterwards Chris Scott was predicting Hawkins, who had struggled with back issues early in his career, would be around for at least a couple more years.

'I think it is possible,' Scott said. 'Our approach is to be open to that possibility and make sure our program reflects that.' He said the common perception of a footballer who had a bad trot after the age of 30 was not that they were sore, or out of form – simply that they were 'too old'. 'We don't subscribe to that,' he declared.

The Cats' coach also gave context to the sluggish performance revealing they'd ramped up a heavy mid-season training block as part of the plan to be peaking in September. The bye had been anything but a week off.

'It's what we do during the middle period of the year. We double down, even more than we might have done in previous years,' Scott said. 'We might cost ourselves a little short-term, but we set up our program to be at our best when it counts. If we finish ninth because we try to prime ourselves to be at our best later in the year, then we'll live with that.

'We haven't been able to execute that over the last few years anyway. That's a reason to do it better.'

CHAPTER 15

Round 15

Saturday June 25, 4.35 pm
Melbourne Cricket Ground
Geelong 13.11.89 versus Richmond 13.8.86

'**C**ATS on the canvas.'

Dwayne Russell in the Fox Footy commentary box captured the moment perfectly. Richmond's Tom Lynch had just kicked the second goal of the final quarter at the five-minute mark to extend the lead to 17 points.

The Tigers fans in the MCG were going berserk as they'd watched their side fight back from 35 points down early in the second quarter to now be in total control of what was being hailed as one of the games of the year, fittingly played before a huge crowd of 59,335, the biggest the Cats had played in front of so far in 2022 – a year when players, fans and everyone else in the game were delighted to be back at the grounds in force after the Covid years.

And this game had already had a bit of everything.

There were surprise late changes by both teams. Richmond dropped ruckman Ivan Soldo to the substitute role in favour of midfielder Hugo Ralphsmith, which meant full-forward Jack Riewoldt had to chop out in the ruck.

Geelong lost Gary Rohan 20 minutes before the opening bounce because of illness, bringing Zach Guthrie into the starting team, which meant the magnets had to be reshuffled, resulting in Jack Henry, who was playing his first game since Round 5, moving forward.

The Cats had controlled the start of the game, kicking the opening two goals through Mark Blicavs and Henry, before an unfortunate incident changed the course of the game and the season of one of Geelong's prime movers.

When Tom Stewart and Dion Prestia came together on the Shane Warne Stand wing – renamed earlier in the year after the champion cricketer died suddenly of natural causes in Thailand – the Cats vice-captain's intention was to block the Richmond midfielder who'd just tapped the ball forward.

Unfortunately he got it badly wrong. Stewart's shoulder hit Prestia flush on the chin, knocking him to the turf where he lay motionless for several moments. Play continued on and shortly after Tyson Stengle kicked another goal for the Cats.

By this time replays of the incident had been shown and the pundits in the stands and elsewhere were playing the guessing game of how many weeks Stewart would get. Stewart himself didn't need to see the replay – he knew he'd stuffed up badly as Prestia was helped off the ground and subsequently ruled out of the game with concussion.

At the quarter-time huddle Stewart was visibly upset. Captain Joel Selwood was having a quiet word with him as Chris Scott made a beeline straight to his star defender when he got down onto the ground. The incident would be debated ad nauseam over the next couple of days, with some commentators immediately calling for a send-off rule to be introduced.

Scott's immediate concern was making sure Stewart found a way to continue contributing for the next three quarters despite the guilt he was feeling. It helped that Geelong were motoring along nicely with goals to Jeremy Cameron, who was playing his 200th game, and things were looking good when Gryan Miers extended the lead out to 35 points 11 minutes into the second quarter.

But there was a reason Richmond had won three flags in the past five years: they knew not to panic, and slowly started to change the flow of the game in the lead-up to half-time. The margin was back to 20 at the main break and then Tigers star Shai Bolton inspired a five-goal-to-one third quarter to grab the lead.

And then when Lynch kicked his third for the night early in the last quarter, Richmond had kicked 10 of the last 12 goals of the game. The Cats needed an answer and they found it in the form of Cameron, but not in the usual way. The key forward went into the centre of the ground and had an impact with several clearances, his brilliant field kicking helping Geelong to get back control of the ball.

It was Stengle, playing against his old team, who turned the tide after Miers found him with a short pass 45 metres out. He nailed the shot – his 29th goal for the season – and a couple of minutes later his partner in crime Brad Close snapped brilliantly across his body to reduce the lead to five points.

Then with 10 minutes left on the clock Stengle was again involved, receiving a wonderful 40-metre pass from Hawkins on his non-preferred left foot which he marked and then immediately played on, handballing over to Cameron who was alone in the goal square. The Cats now led by three points.

They'd got off the canvas.

The intensity and atmosphere was finals-like with both teams trading blows before some individual brilliance by Tigers wingman Marlion Pickett saw him deliver a perfect pass to youngster Maurice Rioli Jnr who marked in the forward pocket. Although still young and green, he was Richmond royalty – his father, Maurice Snr, was a three-time All-Australian and 1982 Norm Smith Medallist during his 118-game career at Punt Road. Elite skill was

Tyson Stengle celebrates a key goal in Round 15.

the family trait and the apple hadn't fallen far from the tree, as the 19-year-old steered through the pressure shot to get his team back in front with just two minutes remaining.

What happened next in many ways encapsulated what was happening at Geelong. The centre clearance didn't come from Selwood or Cam Guthrie; it was Tom Atkins whose left-foot kick rolled dangerously to centre half-forward.

Meeting the ball at full speed was Stengle, who'd charged up from the forward pocket. He then gathered and quickly screwed the ball over his shoulder, sending it to the top of the goal square.

With Richmond players frantically trying to punch it away, it wasn't Hawkins or Cameron who took the match-winning mark. It was regular defender Henry. He then calmly went back and slotted the goal from 15 metres with just 78 seconds remaining.

Three young, relatively inexperienced players had produced the play that won Geelong the best home-and-away game of the season.

However, there was still one last moment of drama with Richmond managing to surge forward again only for their No.1 enemy, Stewart, to take the game-saving mark, his 17th intercept possession of the day. He also recorded a game-high 737 metres gained and a game-high 29 disposals.

Henry revealed afterwards he'd been dealing with a corked thigh leading up to his heroics. 'I copped a pretty big corky early, so I was sort of hobbling a little bit,' he said. '[But] after half-time you're always a bit stiff so I just tried to run out and have a crack. I think when the intensity does lift you kind of get up and go and you don't think too much about how your body is feeling. I had a pretty good look for the run and jump at it, so you've got to go for it. It was very instinctive. The other part wasn't as instinctive so I pretty much tried to hit the foot and got it through.'

Scott made his way onto the ground after the siren and again went to Stewart, who was still clearly upset by the Prestia incident.

'I've known Tom for a long time, he is a scrupulously fair player and just a fantastic, strong character. Fundamental to what we do at Geelong,' Scott said. 'When my time's come and gone I'll look back and say I was honoured to know and to coach Tom Stewart.

'That's partly because when I spoke to him post-game he said, "I've just made a horrible error, and I feel terrible about it. I ran past the ball and I chose to bump. I didn't mean to do it, but gee it was terrible execution, and I'm going to pay the price for it." He knows he's done the wrong thing. Was it deliberate? Of course it wasn't.

'He's made an error and as people do that I admire he's prepared to stand up and say, "I was wrong." He should have some comfort in the fact that that's not him and it was an error in execution and nothing more. He's a pretty emotional guy. He was feeling it and we could see visibly right from the moment it happened.

'And it weighs heavily on him because he's that kind of guy. He referenced letting the team down. He'll pay a price, there's no doubt about that.'

The Cats' coach was quick to add he was against a send-off rule being introduced into the AFL. 'I'm strongly of the view that there shouldn't be match-day reports, because the risk of an umpire getting it wrong is far too great,' Scott said. 'And the idea of sending someone off and getting it wrong in a big game is a risk not worth taking.'

On his side's comeback, in which they recorded 11 consecutive inside 50s to rip back that gap, he said: 'I was really full of admiration for the way they kept backing themselves. The game looked gone a couple of times there and as a collective we didn't play safe.'

That had been a mantra since the start of the season, which was paying dividends. And not playing safe is exactly how Geelong had landed the man who was already the recruit of the year.

Tyson Stengle had been placed in the too hard basket by every other club in 2021 after he was sacked by Adelaide in March that year following a trail of indiscretions, including being caught with cocaine alongside teammate

Brad Crouch, which resulted in being referred to counselling under a drug-diversion program, and drink-driving. His time in Adelaide hadn't worked out. The kid from South Australia's Ceduna, 800 kilometres north-west of Adelaide, had initially been drafted by Richmond in the 2017 Rookie Draft.

While he managed only two games in two years, he was very well liked at Punt Road, but when the Crows came knocking with a three-year contract offer – the Tigers were only offering two – he decided to head home. Two senior games in 2019 were followed by 12 more in 2020 and while there had been flashes of brilliance it wasn't enough to balance out the off-field shenanigans.

After his sacking Stengle turned to SANFL club Woodville West Torrens, where it was obvious to numerous recruiters that he was the best footballer not playing in the AFL that year. But most were too scared to even consider him. Collingwood was the exception, then they got cold feet.

'I was close with Collingwood in the mid-season draft last year, but didn't end up going there,' Stengle said. 'They pulled the pin at the last minute. I am not too sure why. Not too sure what to think about that. Obviously, I missed [being picked] in the mid-season draft then. It was pretty tough. I was a little bit sad, but I forgot about it pretty quick. We had a game that weekend, so I went out and played at the [Woodville West Torrens] Eagles and my goal for the rest of the year was to play good footy each week and go far in the finals with the Eagles.'

Geelong had not yet been in contact, but behind the scenes they were doing their reconnaissance.

On the field Stengle had excelled with Woodville West Torrens, kicking three goals in the Grand Final which the Eagles won easily, while he'd taken steps off the field to get his life in order. There were plenty of people in his corner at Kardinia Park. Assistant coach Shaun Grigg was talking to list manager Andrew Mackie and recruiter Stephen Wells about the goalsneak.

Grigg had played with Stengle at Richmond and loved him as a bloke. Josh Jenkins, who was now the Cats ruck coach, had done the same in Adelaide and also backed in his character. 'He wasn't a bad kid. He had made a few mistakes. From a football point of view it was a no-brainer, but from a character point of view there weren't many issues,' Jenkins said.

And then there was Eddie Betts, the new assistant coach who assured the Cats that he would take Stengle under his wing. 'I said to him, "You are 23. You have got 10 years ahead of you. You can make a life of these 10 years at Geelong,"' Betts said.

The former Carlton and Adelaide star knew more than most about the traumatic and turbulent background surrounding Stengle's upbringing.

Stengle was brought up by his grandmother Debra from the age of four and then by Emily and Cecil Betts, his grandparents on the other side of his family. (While Eddie is related to Cecil Betts he didn't know Tyson in the early days.)

'There's a bit of trauma in my life. Everything happens for a reason, I guess,' Stengle said. 'I am grateful I have got my other family, had my grandmother around, my poppa is still around and then my brother and my sister, so I am grateful for them. Football was always my life growing up. When I stepped out on the footy field I felt safe. I feel good on the footy field.'

The Cats signed Stengle as a delisted free agent and he was soon a favourite among his teammates. He had the nickname 'Wombat' from his Richmond days, because he was so low to the ground, so strong, they just couldn't tackle him. At Adelaide he'd been called 'The President', which Dangerfield knew about and quickly embraced for the new recruit.

'Everyone has weights groups, when you are supposed to do them. He was happy to fall into line early. But very quickly we realised why he has the nickname "The President",' Dangerfield said.

'He does things when he wants to do them and very quickly he found himself doing weights when he likes. He has just had a wonderful season. So much of the commentary has been about what football has given Tyson, but I look at what he has given his teammates, the club and supporters. Everyone has made blues along their journey. There is not a person who exists that hasn't. I think one thing we do as a football club is understand that.'

Dangerfield was amused that Wells wouldn't take a bet that he'd offered early into the pre-season after watching Stengle from close quarters. 'He wouldn't take the bet but I said to Wellsy he will kick 35 goals this year. I was wrong – he's going to get a lot more than that.'

CHAPTER 16

Round 16

Saturday July 2, 7.25 pm

GMHBA Stadium

Geelong 21.18.144 versus North Melbourne 5.2.32

'WE'RE just going to win it aren't we?'

Joel Selwood had made the premiership declaration at the regular coffee catch-up he had with his fellow leaders, vice-captains Patrick Dangerfield and Tom Stewart.

'Yep, we are,' was Dangerfield's reply.

Dangerfield was just relieved that someone else had said it out loud, as it was something he had been sensing for some time. There was a different feel about 2022 – the confidence in the group was brewing, and the new game style was starting to click.

The Cats were sitting second on the ladder, a game behind reigning premiers Melbourne, and hadn't lost a game since Round 9.

In Dangerfield's mind a fit and firing Jeremy Cameron, which hadn't been the case the previous year, changed everything. He could win games off his own boot, while the emergence of Tyson Stengle and the rock-solid greatness of Tom Hawkins made it the most dangerous forward line in the competition. At the other end the man sitting next to him, Stewart, had simply decided in several games this year that the Cats weren't going to lose.

It was a good mix.

'I was always confident if we could be level pegging halfway through the year we'd be fine, because it [the game plan] would be better in the second half of the year than we were in the first because of the adjustments we were making,' Dangerfield said.

'You can't just click your fingers and all of a sudden nail a new style. Even though it was just subtle changes, the new style probably cost us a few games early but it was short-term pain for long-term gain. But once we got it how we needed to play it, then it started to sing.'

Plus there was the Selwood factor.

Dangerfield didn't know if his skipper was going to retire at the end of the season, but he'd started to toss up a few hints which made him think he might be on his farewell tour. 'I did have a quiet moment halfway through the year where I thought, "I can see us winning this thing,"'

Dangerfield said. 'If the footy gods truly exist then if there is one person deserving of it, it's Joel.'

If there are footy gods then there are also injury gods, and they were finally letting Dangerfield loose – or more to the point and back down to earth, Harry Taylor and his medical staff were. They'd deliberately held Danger back for four weeks, one longer than planned, but now he was back.

'I'm competitive, I want to play and watching from the stands – it doesn't satisfy like actually being out there,' Dangerfield said. 'I'll be honest, it took me a little while to wrap my head around it, that this is where it was at.'

He was back, and he didn't take long to announce his return. In fact it took just 13 seconds against North Melbourne for Dangerfield to remind the competition of what he brought to the table.

The Brownlow Medallist started in at the centre bounce and hit the loose ball generated by a Rhys Stanley tap at full speed, then ran to the edge of the square and unloaded a 55-metre drop punt which bounced through to send the Cats faithful into hysterics.

He'd replaced Selwood in the team, who was on his scheduled rest, while key defender Sam De Koning was also being managed. As expected, Stewart was missing. The pundits who had guessed he'd get four weeks were right.

Immediately after the Richmond match the previous week, the Cats defender had reached out to Richmond's Dion Prestia to apologise.

'Nothing that I can say now justifies the actions that I showed on the day, but my immediate response was to just make sure Dion was OK,' Stewart said. 'I reached out to him immediately after the game. [Jack] Riewoldt gave me his number, and he was in good spirits. He understood that there was no malicious intent and it was a poor decision by me. It was [a tough conversation]. Nothing makes it easier, but the way that he understood that my intent wasn't to maliciously hurt him and the way it happened wasn't directly meant for him, made me feel a little bit more at ease. But it still sits in my gut and still makes me feel quite ill.'

The bottom-of-the-ladder Kangaroos were themselves feeling very ill after quarter-time, as it was all one-way traffic for the Cats, who kicked 18 goals to two to inflict on North its biggest loss of the season – 112 points.

It was brutal. Hawkins kicked six goals while Cameron was best on ground again with 4.3 goals from 30 disposals, which included 10 marks. Stengle, Quinton Narkle and Brad Close each kicked two goals, while Mitch Duncan celebrated his 250th game with 30 disposals.

One interesting sideline to the thrashing was the ruck duel between Stanley and Todd Goldstein. The Cats tried to extract Goldstein from Arden Street in 2019 but failed. The ruck position at Kardinia Park had been a constant focus of debate among fans since the halcyon days of Brad Ottens, whose last game was the 2011 Grand Final.

Since Stanley arrived via a trade at the end of 2014 after 58 games with St Kilda, there have been plenty of challengers for his spot come through the doors, including Zac Smith, Ryan Abbott and Darcy Fort. Hawthorn ruckman Jonathon Ceglar was brought in in 2021 during the trade period but he'd been struck down with injury and hadn't yet shown his hand.

Through it all Stanley, who was playing his 116th game for the Cats against North Melbourne, had kept fronting up despite the noise around his role.

'I'm sort of concerned about the stuff internally not really externally. I don't read a thing, I don't watch anything,' Stanley said. 'I don't read it as it gets my nose out of joint a bit when I read a lot of it, so I just leave it.

'I think the ones that know are inside the walls here, so they are the ones I trust and listen to. Scotty has been great for me, he has always had my back and we've got a great relationship. [Assistant coach] Nigel Lappin has done a lot of work with me and has been fantastic as well over the journey.

'I don't know if there is any added pressure, I find that pressure in any footy club. The ruck is not an easy position to play, you are sort of one out, you are out there in the middle and all eyes are on you. You have got to perform and when you don't you come under fire.'

Stanley was left out of the side an hour before the qualifying final against Collingwood in 2019, a decision which backfired on coach Chris Scott as Pies ruckman Brodie Grundy then proceeded to lead his team to victory.

Stanley's body has previously let him down at inappropriate times, which has been more fuel for the critics, and there have been times like 2021 when he was stranded in the VFL. His number seemed to be up – but he got back up again and fought back.

'There are always revolving doors, people coming and going all the time at footy clubs, conversations being had constantly,' he said. 'I've been in and out of the side a little bit. Last year was not too bad but the year before it was sort of inconsistent. I was playing some good footy and then I would just have games where I was very inconsistent. I've also figured out the body a bit. The body is feeling better as I have gotten older.

'I did seven hammies in two years when I was young. That's a pain in the arse, it sucks, you just don't trust anything, you just don't trust your body, so that was frustrating. The medical team here, the strength and conditioning team, we did a heap of work and I feel like it is starting to pay off.'

A change in philosophy away from continually worrying about his spot in the team had resulted in a new freedom in 2022. 'I think I just got a handle on what was important, and what was important within my role, and it was keeping things simple and helping the guy next to me,' Stanley said.

'So that's a bit of the mantra for the last year or two – it's what can I do for the guy next to me rather than myself. What can I do to let those guys do what they do? That has worked pretty well this year.'

Stanley did plenty to help his teammates do as they pleased against North, taking care of Goldstein in their head-to-head battle having 17 disposals, seven marks and 25 hit-outs compared to his rival's disappointing seven touches and 15 hit-outs.

CHAPTER 17

Round 17

Thursday July 7, 7.20 pm

GMHBA Stadium

Geelong 12.19.91 versus Melbourne 9.9.63

THE passionate Chris Scott fist pump told the story.

The moment wasn't one of your after-the-siren goals to win the match – it was simply a moment halfway through the second quarter in a late-season game. But it was the moment that all the pre-season training, all the meetings, all the video watching had come together in one passage of play that epitomised the 2022 version of Geelong.

Zach Tuohy had the kick-in after a Melbourne behind, playing on into the back pocket before firing a 40-metre pass onto the chest of ruckman Rhys Stanley. Rather than look down the line where the Demons were beginning to set up their defensive wall, he turned inside and delivered a beautiful kick across the centre square to Max Holmes.

Holmes played on immediately, but instead of going long and playing into the hands of Melbourne's intercept kings, Steven May and Jake Lever, he lowered his eyes and found Cam Guthrie just inside the centre square. He didn't waste any time either, but gave a quick handball to Mitch Duncan, who did the same to Joel Selwood. He then delivered another lightning-quick handball to the running Isaac Smith, who with excellent vision handballed sideways to Gryan Miers in space.

With the Demons' wall broken, Miers had time to deliver a long handball to Brad Close, who was alone in the forward pocket. He then calmly strolled in from 15 metres out and kicked the goal of Geelong's season. It was poetry in motion for Scott and his coaching staff, who celebrated accordingly in the box.

The Thursday night contest at GMHBA Stadium had a finals feel about it and there was no doubt a theme of exorcising past demons for the Geelong players after 2021's preliminary final loss. They knew winning in Round 17 didn't wipe that away, but if their new game style stood up against the best team in the competition then it meant a lot for what they wanted to achieve in a couple of months' time.

The pre-game focus had been about winning the ball at the coalface against Melbourne. That was their strength, along with their intercept defenders, so the Cats set about a plan to at least match them in these areas. A refreshed Patrick Dangerfield was the key to this, along with Tom Atkins, Selwood and Guthrie, while Mark Blicavs was helping out in the ruck, then diving straight into the play where he was put to use to blunt Norm Smith Medallist Christian Petracca.

A dominant start to the third quarter had the Cats 23 points up when Smith celebrated his 250th game with a trademark long bomb on the run from 50 metres out at the 18-minute mark. All of this had been done without the Cats' big forwards having any say – Tom Hawkins, Jeremy Cameron and Tyson Stengle were all goalless to three-quarter time, as the focus on finding other avenues to goal – and avoiding May and Lever – was working.

However, some wasteful kicking for goal – Dangerfield was the main culprit with four behinds – kept Melbourne in the contest and, like good sides do, they came again. The Demons, who'd started the year with 10 straight wins but had won only two of five games since, kicked four of the next five goals to close within a kick midway through the final term.

If there was still any baggage from last year then this is when it would surface, but the new Geelong steadied, kicking the final three goals of the game to seal a 28-point victory and take over top spot on the AFL ladder. The big guns in the midfield had come to play. Dangerfield was best on ground with 31 disposals, nine clearances, eight inside 50s and a whopping 702 metres gained.

Atkins had been enormous in the clinches with 21 disposals, nine tackles and nine clearances, while Guthrie (28 disposals, seven tackles) and Duncan (32 disposals, 11 marks, 629 metres gained) had both hit the scoreboard with two goals each. Smith had celebrated his 250th milestone in superb style with 22 disposals, seven marks and 382 metres gained. But there was almost as much pleasure in what Geelong denied Melbourne.

The Cats won the clearances 54-36, Petracca having just two clearances for the match. Ruckman Max Gawn, who so often has been an impassable wall, did not take a single intercept mark for the night and finished with just one intercept possession. May managed just three intercept possessions – his second-lowest tally of the season – as he was kept busy by Hawkins.

Geelong's territory wins eventually broke the Demons' defence – they won inside-50s 66-46 – with the Cats scoring 41 points from forward-half chains in the second half. The Demons had conceded just 28.1 points per game from opposition forward-half chains going into the game.

Scott was beaming after a contest he referred to as being an 'audit' of Geelong's evolution. The Cats had lost to the Demons in each of the three matches the previous year, including that preliminary final hiding.

'What it means at the moment is much more important than anything from previous years,' Scott said. 'It was put to me that Simon Goodwin said during the week this game's probably a bit of an audit for where his team's at and we thought that's a pretty good description. Whatever happens, we will learn a bit. We won't get carried away with the win. It doesn't make us the best team in the comp, because we beat them at home. But what it does say to our players is the things we've been working on can stand up against the very best teams.'

When asked about that special play in the second quarter that resulted in the Close goal, Scott said: 'You have to play what the opposition presents in front of you. I think 15, 20 years ago back when the game was much more simple, you could say "we're just going to play this way all the time". Today you can't. If you play that way, you'll get picked apart by good coaching and good opposition teams.

'But in principle, we are trying to challenge the opposition a little bit more – and I think it's a no-brainer when it comes to playing Melbourne. If you're, in effect, saying to Lever or May "you guys get set and when you're ready we'll go forward", it's probably going to be a hard night for you offensively.

'So I thought that [goal] was a good example. We wanted to have a swing at it. And if we failed, we wanted to say "at least we had a crack at what we're trying to execute" as opposed to playing safe – and that's a part our coaching group were pleased about.

'We had a crack early at some of those plays where the Demons looked pretty set and we really challenged them and then when we came late, the easy thing would've been to try to hang on and play really safe footy and I didn't think we did that, which was pleasing.'

There was a clear shift for everyone at Geelong over the next couple of days as the players reflected on the job they'd done on the reigning premier. The data told the coaches everything they wanted to know, but more importantly it was in the minds of the players where James Kelly thought something had clicked.

'It was like the monkey was off the back a little bit,' Kelly said. 'We'd been practising and talking about moving the ball off the line when going forward and that was the game we did it. For them to see that we are doing it against a really good team, who we put to the sword a little bit, the boys were like "Yeah this works." It was like they thought, "We are good to go now" because if we did it against them, we can do it against anyone.

'There was certainly a different feel afterwards and it was almost like there was a new sheriff in town.'

CHAPTER 18

Round 18

Saturday July 16, 7.25 pm
Melbourne Cricket Ground
Geelong 12.13.85 versus Carlton 8.7.55

ALL the hype in the lead-up to this encounter was about the Coleman Medal shoot-out – the top four contenders were all playing in the same game.

This was an extremely rare event, like Halley's Comet for goal-kicking aficionados. The big four, head-to-head, at opposite ends of the ground in a game that had major ramifications for the finals. In the navy corner there was this year's leader Charlie Curnow and last year's winner Harry McKay, while in the blue and white corner were the current second and third placegetters on the table, Jeremy Cameron and Tom Hawkins. Ironically by the end of it all, it was the Geelong defenders who were making the headlines.

The Sam De Koning bandwagon got a few more passengers wanting to get on board after he took McKay to the cleaners, holding him to just one behind. After being beaten by Curnow in the first quarter, De Koning switched with Jack Henry and came into his own, beating McKay in one-on-one duels, out-marking him even though he was conceding 10 cm and 13 kg, and even leading him to the ball.

His rapid development had him now in the conversation with Collingwood young gun Nick Daicos for the AFL Rising Star Award, the pair rated clearly out in front by bookmakers with daylight to the rest.

Henry had almost been out of sight out of mind in 2022, apart from that cameo up forward in Round 15 when he kicked the winning goal against Richmond. Off-season surgery on a partial foot fracture saw him miss the start of the season and then complications with the same injury resulted in him being sidelined for 10 weeks through the middle of the season. Suddenly his shock second-placing in the 2021 Carji Greeves Medal seemed like a lifetime ago. Henry, 23, was pipped by just two votes by fellow defender Tom Stewart for the honour of being named Geelong's best player in 2021. It was a stunning achievement for a player who was overlooked in the 2016 National Draft after an inconsistent season with the Geelong Falcons.

Henry was an athlete playing football. He'd been an elite junior on the track, finishing third in the decathlon at the 2015 Australian junior championships. As a result his skills were questionable, and while he'd made the Vic Country team in the national championships, he didn't do anything to catch the eye.

What was there was clear athleticism: he was 194 cm and agile, which was what attracted Geelong recruiter Stephen Wells to take the local lad with pick No.16 in the Rookie Draft. It would prove to be a pivotal week for the Cats, who a few days earlier at the National Draft had snared Brandan Parfitt (pick No.26), Stewart (No.40), Esava Ratugolea (No.43), Quinton Narkle (No.60) and Ryan Abbott (No.69).

Henry, who had played on the wing and half-forward with the Falcons, toiled away in the VFL in his first season before getting a surprise call-up in the second game of the 2018 season to cover for premiership defender Harry Taylor. Despite having barely played in defence, Henry was thrown in the deep end and managed to stay afloat. He played 22 games that year and with the help of assistant coach Matthew Scarlett he became a permanent fixture.

However, a snub in 2021 when he wasn't selected for the season-opener spurred on Henry's career-best year. While Geelong were being upset by the Adelaide Crows at the Adelaide Oval, Henry was playing in a VFL practice match at Deakin Reserve, before some tough love from Scarlett shocked him into action.

'I remember sitting down early days that pre-season with "Scarlo" and he wanted to be a bit harder on me to take my game to another level,' Henry said. 'It was always, like it would be for everyone, the intention to get better and maybe that was just a way of that tough love.

'I definitely think, in terms of not being complacent with my game, it's definitely helped me and just wanting to be better and wanting to do things that ultimately will help the team rather than just go through my career being at the one level. I still want to keep getting better and better.'

Geelong needed Henry to make the defence better against the Blues after the quarter-time swap with De Koning. He once again delivered when called on, limiting Curnow after he'd kicked two of the Blues' four goals in the opening quarter.

The Coleman Medal leader kicked Carlton's only goal of the second quarter – and that was it for him and his team, who only managed three goals after half-time as the Cats turned the screws on the wannabe finalist.

At the other end Cameron had proved a handful for ex-Bulldog Lewis Young, floating around the MCG collecting 18 disposals and kicking 3.3, including the best goal of the night, a trademark over-the-shoulder snap from 40 metres out against the boundary line. Hawkins was matched up on Jacob Weitering and while it wasn't a spectacular night for him, he still kicked two goals and had an influence.

For Chris Scott the performance of De Koning, who had played 15 of 16 games this year, showed the benefit from not being thrown to the wolves. 'Eighteen-year-old 200-cm key defenders getting towelled up by gun key forwards, I'm not sure how often that's good for them,' Scott said. 'We're not saying it's a beautiful plan that's come together but virtually all the credit should go to Sam himself. He's an overnight success that took three years.'

The wash-up of the Coleman Medal shoot-out with five rounds remaining had Curnow moving to 53 goals, four ahead of Cameron on 49 with Hawkins up to 45.

CHAPTER 19

Round 19

Saturday July 23, 4.35 pm
Adelaide Oval
Geelong 16.10.106 versus Port Adelaide 14.10.94

A S far as Geelong goes, there is no bigger compliment.

'Tom Atkins in this quarter – I know he's announced himself in the last 10 weeks as a genuine bona fide midfielder – he's now announced himself as a Selwood-like matchwinner when something needed to be done,' Melbourne great and Fox Footy commentator Garry Lyon said. 'He's been incredible.'

To put into perspective one of the best quarters of football played by an individual in 2022, what happened in the previous 90 minutes needs some context. In the lead-up a lot had been made about the last time Geelong clashed with Port Adelaide at Adelaide Oval. It had been in the previous year's qualifying final and the Cats got smacked by 43 points. This time around the Power were fighting for their lives to stay in the finals race, the scenario being that they had to win to stay alive.

After an even opening term, it was the Cats who gained the ascendancy in the second quarter, mainly through a dominant display from ruckman Rhys Stanley, who exploited Port's plan to not go with a specialist big man, instead using forwards Jeremy Finlayson and Charlie Dixon in the ruck. Stanley had 12 disposals (10 contested), eight clearances, 16 hit-outs and three score involvements to be clearly the most influential player on the ground.

The Cats kicked six goals to one in the second quarter, and included in the onslaught was a contender for worst miss of the year, when Jeremy Cameron ran into an open goal only for his dribble kick to bounce across the face. Just before the half-time siren Port's defence offered up its contender for clanger of the day after a comedy of errors saw Power defender Ryan Burton drill an attempted clearing kick onto the chest of Isaac Smith. He then went back and slotted a beautiful set shot from 50 metres out to extend the margin to 34 points.

However, the game changed dramatically in the third quarter after a knee injury to Stanley, who was substituted off, replaced by 19-year-old ruckman Shannon Neale, who was playing just his second game.

Port Adelaide went on a rampage, dominating the centre of the ground, with Finlayson feeding his midfielders, who were running in waves. The result was eight goals to one, to lead by seven points at the final change. It had been breathtaking from the home side and left Geelong searching for answers.

At least the three-quarter time break gave the visitors a chance to reset. Atkins won the first centre clearance of the final quarter, which resulted in a goal to Cameron inside 15 seconds. The Cats got the lead back seven minutes later when Mitch Duncan showed terrific composure, delivering a lovely ball inside 50 to Tyson Stengle for his first goal of the afternoon.

There was controversy soon after when Patrick Dangerfield and Port's Aliir Aliir chased a ball dribbling towards Geelong's goal-line. Aliir dived head-first and Dangerfield lunged feet-first, appearing to get his boot studs to the ball just before it crossed the goal-line. But the goal umpire signalled a point, and despite Dangerfield's appeals, play continued without a video check from the AFL's review system.

Enter Tom Hawkins. Once again he came up clutch, kicking two goals in two minutes to ice the game.

A perfectly weighted kick by Brad Close set up the first opportunity with four-and-a-half minutes remaining. Hawkins managed to push away Port defender Tom Clurey and mark on his chest. He then went back and calmly slotted a left-foot snap set shot from 15 metres.

It was his ruck craft a minute later that saw the Cats' full-forward awarded a free kick for over the shoulder. Hawkins was 45 metres out on a 45-degree angle but these big shots in big moments were his bread and butter – the kick sailed straight over the umpire's cap.

Geelong had done it again. The new steel and resolve of Chris Scott's team had risen again, getting them up from being down on their knees to win one of the games of the season. How did they do it? There was one easy answer – Atkins.

The unheralded rookie carried Geelong on his shoulders in an epic final term, in which he collected a game-high 12 disposals, seven contested possessions, two clearances and executed 31 pressure acts. Former Collingwood coach Nathan Buckley agreed with Lyon's praise on Fox Footy: 'He finds the ball, but it's not about that, it's about impact. When the ball needs to be won, he's the one who's done it.'

With Joel Selwood and Dangerfield having relatively quiet games – they only had 24 possessions between them – Atkins became the Cats' general, collecting 24 disposals, five clearances and a team-high seven tackles.

Afterwards a modest Atkins said he was still 'on the fringe' of Geelong's best 22. 'I don't care where I play, I'm just happy to be in the 22 at the moment,' he said. 'There are a lot of great guys in the VFL that are missing out at the moment, so I think we owe it to them to play well – I owe it to them because I'm on the fringe. So I'm just happy that we're able to win.'

Buckley praised Atkins' attitude as 'a dog-hungry type player where you get sort of that response and performance in the last quarter'. Lyon went further to point at Atkins' pathway through Geelong's VFL side via the Rookie Draft as a lesson to rival club scouts.

'If you're a recruiter out there or you're a side that hasn't competed in finals for a while and you're sitting there bemoaning the fact your list is not that great and you've only got access to X amount of draft picks – exhibit A, right there, the Geelong No.30,' Lyon said.

'You're going through the qualities of the players you want, but if in doubt go for dog-hungry competitors every single time – and that's what he is. I would defy anyone that didn't sit back and enjoy watching him in that last quarter and his last eight weeks since going into the middle of the ground.'

Scott had been in the best seat in the house to watch Atkins flourish since the midfield move, which he pointed out was a result of the fresh new direction of his coaching panel. 'He's just been terrific for us without surprising us,' Scott said. 'Especially Shaun Grigg, working with him really closely. James Kelly, working a bit more with our defenders, sort of identified some things that would work in the midfield. It's nice for those guys when a plan comes together. It probably speaks a little bit to the system we have. We don't have a territorial group of assistant coaches. When the back guys help the midfield guys with one of the guys that's in really good form, I think it's a good sign.'

Atkins' teammates were lining up to praise one of the most respected players at the club. 'He just gives us a different dynamic,' Hawkins said. 'He's been so versatile in his career at Geelong – he's played forward with us for a period then down back and here he comes to play in the midfield. He's been excellent, but I think he's typifying the way we're playing at the moment, executing his role really well and he's getting the reward for it.'

Duncan probably summed it up for all of them: 'He is one of the toughest players I have come across, even when he was involved in the VFL system and he used to train with us, I used to avoid him all the time and I still do now.'

CHAPTER 20

Round 20

Saturday July 30, 7.25 pm

GMHBA Stadium

Geelong 14.10.94 versus Western Bulldogs 9.12.66

'H E'S the best player I've seen in my time.'

By his own admission Chris Scott was emotional in the lead-up to Joel Selwood's 350th game, in which the Cats' skipper became only the 21st player in AFL/VFL history to reach the milestone. You might think a club with 21 members is not that exclusive, but more than 13,000 have played AFL or VFL – which puts Selwood in the top 0.0003 per cent.

Scott played with Brownlow medallists Michael Voss, Simon Black and Jason Akermanis in a premiership golden era at the Brisbane Lions, but rates Selwood on a pedestal above them and anyone else.

'I feel so privileged to have worked with such a great captain,' Scott said. 'I think the positional comparisons are hard, but I'll just say it, and I think I've said it before, that I find it hard to compare eras, but he's the best player I've seen in my time when you take everything into consideration. In terms of impact on a football club and assistance to a head coach, I can't think of any better.

'I'm still pinching myself every day walking into the Geelong footy club. It'd be nice to be able to tell my kids and grandkids one day that I spent a lot of time with Joel Selwood. It's a real privilege.'

Selwood's best mate Tom Hawkins was adamant – the Cats' games record holder was also its best ever player.

Patrick Dangerfield wasn't holding back in his praise either. 'Blood dripping down from the eye, screaming and pointing. I just picture that when I think of him,' Dangerfield said. 'He's a gladiator on the field. He always stands up in big moments, he's super consistent, his ceiling is extraordinary. But then, he's an even better person. You think it isn't fair to have someone tick every box.'

In the lead-up to the milestone game against the Western Bulldogs, which was fittingly being played at the ground where it all started way back in November 2006, the 34-year-old was still coming to terms with the enormity of the achievement.

'I'm actually not sure how to put it,' Selwood said. 'A couple of weeks ago when Scott Pendlebury made the milestone and I saw how big the occasion was for the

Collingwood footy club, it made me understand that it's probably going to be bigger than I thought.

'[And] I appreciate that others will enjoy it too. I've always understood how old the footy club is, I've loved that aspect of it. I barracked for the Cats as a kid and never dreamt of going on to play this many games, but the journey has been so fun and I think that's what has made it all go so fast.'

The journey almost never happened. Selwood was told by doctors when he was 17 that the persistent knee injury that had plagued his junior years was so bad he wouldn't be able to play AFL football. He would go under the knife four times before his 18th birthday, and after the fourth operation, the surgeon delivered some crushing news.

'We'd tried to do something with it in Bendigo to fix it, but it didn't work out,' Selwood's father, Bryce, recalled. 'So we went down to Melbourne and the surgeon indicated that someone undergoing this operation would have the use of his knee, but that there was the likelihood that he'd never play sport at an elite level.'

According to his mother, Maree, hearing that news was one of the few times she saw Joel cry. 'Joel was a real rough nut as a kid and you really had to hurt him to make him cry. He'd hardly cry, but he came home that day and there were tears,' Maree said. 'I remember saying to him, "Joel, you can do it, let's prove the surgeon wrong," and giving him all the right words to turn those tears into determination. And that's exactly what he did.'

As the Geelong Football Club tell it, he'd grown up with three brothers – older twins Adam and Troy, and younger sibling Scott – in Strathdale, a suburb 3 kilometres east of the Bendigo city centre, where they'd hone their football skills around the light post out the front of their house. Whether your weapon of choice was a banana, a torp, a drop punt or a snap, the challenge was the same: hit the post. And the prize? Five red frogs. The boys would battle it out until the sun dipped below the horizon and Maree would call them in for dinner.

This competitive fire that was drilled into him during the backyard tussles with his brothers is what captured the attention of Geelong premiership captain Cameron Ling when he first met Selwood. As part of the then Australian Institute of Sport AFL Academy, the best young players in the land got the opportunity to train for a week with AFL clubs.

'We generally got any [Geelong] Falcons kids who made the Academy or country kids would end up here,' Ling said. 'We got a kid from Bendigo named Joel Selwood, who came and trained with us for a week in 2006. It is fair to say that I and most other senior players quickly went and visited Stephen Wells and asked about the likelihood of us ending up with Joel even after that week. He didn't go out there and have 30 touches in a 15-minute drill, but it just looked like we were watching a bloke who'd been training with us for three years and was on our list.'

Selwood barely played for the Bendigo Pioneers during his draft year because of the knee problem, which scared a number of clubs off, much to the delight of Wells. He went to the 2006 National Draft with two players in mind for his No.7 selection – a local lad from Torquay named Travis Boak and Selwood.

When Port Adelaide took Boak at No.5, it left Hawthorn as the only stumbling block for Wells' plan. Much to his delight, they opted for Tasmanian tall forward Mitch Thorp at No.6 (he played only two games for the Hawks before being delisted in 2009), which allowed the player who would become one of the game's greats to fall into Geelong's lap.

Selwood made his debut in the opening round of the 2007 season and was a permanent fixture from then on, playing 21 games in his debut season, including the record-breaking premiership win over Port Adelaide. And the knee has never been a problem. The opposite in fact – Selwood has been extremely durable across the years.

He did have an early problem in his milestone game as the Western Bulldogs seemed intent on spoiling the party, kicking the opening four goals of the game to silence the capacity home crowd.

By half-time some normality had resumed, with the Dogs' lead cut to 11 points before Selwood's teammates decided it was time to show their appreciation of the skipper.

Four goals in nine minutes at the start of the third quarter – two from Hawkins – got the party started with a blistering 8.3 to 0.3 for the term finishing off the Dogs. With Tom Stewart returning for his first game back from his four-week ban, the Cats' defence was impenetrable: the Dogs went 50 minutes of game time – from just before half-time to midway through the final quarter – without kicking a goal.

Geelong had 18 inside 50s to six in the third quarter as Dangerfield wound back the clock, gathering eight touches in the term and bulldozing his way over the Bulldogs. Sitting on the interchange bench, his former Adelaide teammate Josh Jenkins, who was now the Cats' ruck coach, was relieved and excited. His mate was back.

As the team came in for the three-quarter time huddle, Jenkins went straight over to his friend. 'That is the Pat of old,' he whispered in Dangerfield's ear.

Danger finished with best-on-ground honours thanks to a powerhouse 26 disposals, 10 contested possessions and seven score involvements in what turned into a comfortable 28-point victory.

'His weapon is to go and hunt the ball and we've seen him as a younger man dive on the ball, have two or three blokes hanging off him, and just stand up,' Jenkins said afterwards. 'We saw a display of athleticism that, I'll be honest, I wasn't 100 per cent sure was still under the hood. As a 32-year-old with a lot of tread coming up on game 300 ... I wasn't sure.

'It was the beast feeding itself in that term. The more he did it, the more the chest was puffed out. We've seen him at his absolute best. He's probably had periods this season where he's doubted himself a little bit. He still is [a physical beast].'

Ex-Hawk Jonathon Ceglar made his long-awaited debut as replacement for the injured Rhys Stanley, while midfielder Brandan Parfitt played his first game after missing eight weeks with a hand injury, coming on as the medical sub after Gary Rohan was concussed in the last quarter.

It was the Cats' 10th win on the trot, and it kept Selwood's milestone game strike-rate intact. He had now played in a winning team in every milestone match, from 50 games to 350 (and for that matter the Round 3 game against Collingwood when he became the longest-serving captain in the history of the game).

With family and friends on the ground, Selwood was chaired off by Hawkins and Mitch Duncan through a guard of honour that included the Bulldogs players and every Geelong staff member.

Rather than go straight down into the rooms, Selwood turned and ran back to the centre of the ground by himself to acknowledge the fans. It was a powerful image, the great warrior going to the four points of the centre square, clapping and waving to the people who'd had his back for the past 16 years.

AFL legend Leigh Matthews was watching the touching moment and instantly thought there might be more to it. 'Joel Selwood post-game on Saturday night ... when he walked around the centre square to acknowledge the crowd, I thought to myself, "That looked like a player who was saying goodbye,"' Matthews said.

'I just wonder what's in Joel's mind, whether he's not sure whether he'll continue on. "They're celebrating my 350th game, I now have a chance to in a way thank and celebrate with the Geelong fans that might never happen again." That was an observation that popped into my mind when Joel was doing that lap of honour.'

Selwood wasn't giving too much away when quizzed about whether he'd try to become just the sixth player in VFL/AFL history to reach 400 games.

For the moment, there was only one thing on his mind. 'I sometimes let the mind wander,' he admitted. 'But to be honest it's only to the end of the season and lifting up that premiership cup.'

CHAPTER 21

Round 21

Saturday August 6, 7.25 pm

GMHBA Stadium

Geelong 17.8.110 versus St Kilda 10.5.65

STEPHEN Wells knew it was a punt, but if ever there was a year to take one it was in the 2020 National Draft.

With the Covid pandemic having thrown football competitions around the country into disarray, the recruiters were running on limited information, given the players hadn't been able to compete for almost the entire year, and the recruiters had even less chance to see them. It was almost a throwback to the good old days where you had to rely a bit on word of mouth and an ability to see into the future.

One of Wells' contacts had reached out about a kid he'd coached in U/16s who was raw – but there was something there that he needed to look into.

ROUND 17: WIN
This was an important win against the reigning premiers, the Melbourne Demons. The Cats moved into the top spot on the ladder on percentage, dislodging Melbourne. They had a lot to celebrate after the game.

ROUND 18: WIN
Carlton were recognised as a formidable force, sitting just outside the four in fifth place on the ladder. Geelong's win sent Carlton to seventh place behind Sydney. Here, Jack Henry fights for the ball during the Carlton match.

ROUND 19: WIN

Port Adelaide, playing at home, had Geelong in their sights after half-time. At three-quarter time it was a make or break moment with Port Adelaide in the lead by seven points. Whatever was said in that final huddle turned the game around with Geelong winning by 12 points.

ROUND 20: WIN

Geelong were in the top spot on the ladder on points now. But it was getting to the pointy end of the season and they were back playing the Western Bulldogs, who had been unpredictable most of the year. It was also their captain's 350th game. They needed to win it and they did.

ROUND 21: WIN
Geelong had found their winning form and just needed to hold on to it in these last pressing rounds – and they did, comfortably beating St Kilda. Zach Tuohy plays his part as he prepares to pass the ball in the match against St Kilda.

ROUND 22: WIN
The game against Gold Coast resulted in a regulation 10-goal win – but the story of the night was the hamstring injury that had Jeremy Cameron finish the game on the bench.

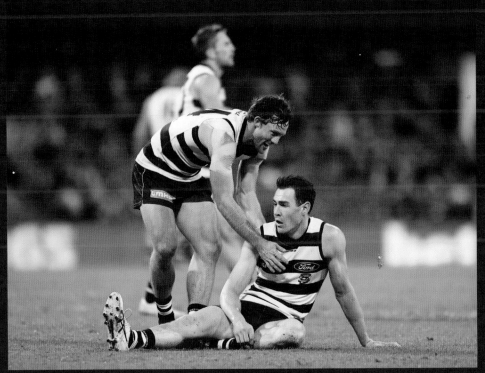

ROUND 23: WIN

The final round before the finals and there are still battles going on with four clubs on equal points behind Geelong. Geelong headed off West Coast to stay on top ahead of Melbourne, Sydney and Collingwood. But it was Patrick Dangerfield's 300th game to celebrate as well.

FIRST QUALIFYING FINAL: WIN

In front of 91,525 fans, the Cats were behind Collingwood at every change but kicked four of the last five goals to win an absolute thriller. With level scores and only 1:20 minutes left, Max Holmes kicked the match-winner (RIGHT).

BELOW: The team line-up for the First Qualifying Final in 2022.

FIRST PRELIMINARY FINAL: WIN

Gary Rohan kicks the ball away in the First Preliminary Final. With their confidence buoyed by the previous win, Geelong hit Brisbane with everything they had and won by 71 points to demolish any thoughts that the Cats were too old and too slow. The Grand Final awaited them.

GRAND FINAL

ABOVE: The team photo.

RIGHT: Geelong legend, Gary Ablett Jr. with his little boy, Levi, before Joel Selwood carried Levi onto the ground.

BELOW LEFT: At the 14 minute mark Sydney were scoreless – a sign of things to come.

BELOW RIGHT: Jeremy Cameron and Tom Hawkins celebrate a goal with teammates. Both came equal third in the Coleman Medal with 59 goals.

TOP: Although being tackled by Swans player Braedon Campbell, Patrick Dangerfield went on to handball the ball away.

MIDDLE: Joel Selwood moves the ball forward as Sydney feel the pressure mount.

LEFT: Emotion overtakes Joel Selwood after kicking a late goal in the last game of his career.

TOP LEFT: The team congratulates Isaac Smith after he is named the Norm Smith Medallist.

TOP RIGHT: Joel Selwood shares the win with their popular water boy Sam Moorfoot.

MIDDLE: Coach and captain raise the cup.

BOTTOM: The team gather for a winning photo.

His name was Max Holmes.

He certainly had the athletic breeding given he was the son of Lee Naylor, an Olympic 400-metre runner and Australian teammate of the great Cathy Freeman. It was no surprise that Holmes had followed in his mother's footsteps and shown serious promise, winning the Australian under-18 400-metre hurdles title and also finishing third in the 400-metre. But he kept coming back to football, playing for Melbourne Grammar in the Associated Public Schools competition, while also featuring in some trial games with the Sandringham Dragons.

He did play one NAB League game with the Dragons as a bottom-ager, but a broken arm suffered during a school game threw a spanner in the works and he missed most of 2019.

There was an impressive pre-season game before Covid hit and by this time Holmes was in the middle of a growth spurt, resulting in 12 cm being added since the last time any of the recruiters would have seen him play football. As expected, he produced outstanding fitness test results in the lead-up to the draft, which elevated him onto the radar of a number of AFL clubs.

Wells was already convinced the elite runner was worth a speculative pick, but his first selection wasn't until No.33, as the Cats had given away their first-round pick as part of the Jeremy Cameron mega trade.

The veteran recruiter knew there were some clubs sniffing around Holmes, so he made a deal with Richmond, acquiring their selection No.20 in return for the Cats' future first-round pick in 2021.

In keeping with the bizarre year, the draft was held via Zoom for the first time and went for an excruciating three-and-a-half hours to select 59 players.

Wells was understandably nervous, as he knew Holmes was an old-fashioned punt. If he was new to this game, he probably wouldn't have taken the punt, but there was something about the kid that nagged at him. He had all the attributes to be a successful player – the running ability, competitiveness and elite sport mentality. So Wells went with his gut at No.20.

For someone who'd hardly played any football in the previous three years, Holmes quickly started to turn heads at Geelong and made his debut in Round 3, 2021. While there were three games where he was the unused medical sub, at the end of the year the 19-year-old was in the starting 22 for the semi-final and preliminary final.

What most stood out for Cats fans was who he looked like in the No.9 jumper. Holmes was a spitting image for James Kelly, the three-time premiership hero who wore that number in 273 games.

A syndesmosis injury in Round 7 against Fremantle saw him sidelined for two months, but he'd started to find his feet again, which St Kilda – the last team to beat the Cats – found out the hard way.

On paper, the Cats were vulnerable in the Round 21 clash given the spate of withdrawals that had occurred right up to the opening bounce.

Captain Joel Selwood was ruled out on Thursday night as part of his management program, while Gary Rohan missed because of concussion protocols. There were then two other changes: Mark Blicavs was managed as well, while ruckman Jonathon Ceglar also came out of the selected 22 and was named as medical sub. They were replaced by experienced duo Zach Tuohy and Sam Menegola. But there was more drama to come with Patrick Dangerfield in the final 30 minutes leading up to the start of the game.

During the warm-up Dangerfield was in deep discussion with the club's medical staff after feeling tightness in the same calf that saw him miss five games earlier in the season. No risks were taken and he was withdrawn from the side, replaced by Luke Dahlhaus.

'It just got a bit tight – and then given the last time I re-aggravated my calf, to be honest I just didn't trust myself to make the right decision so close to game time,' Dangerfield said. 'At this time of the year, given the situation we're in, the conservative route is the best path forward.

'It'd been a bit tight during the week, even though I trained fully, so I was confident in that regard. But then a bit of deceleration tonight, it just didn't feel right. In the back of your mind it's just ... around making the mature decision around where we're at and where the season's at.'

Geelong had 10 of the first 11 inside 50s for the game but wasted a number of opportunities in front of goal before Tom Hawkins found his radar, kicking two of his side's six goals for the opening term. St Kilda, who were fighting for a spot in the final eight, found their game kicking three of the first four goals of the second quarter.

The margin was 10 points the home side's way at half-time, but the Cats soon ended the contest, kicking four goals in the third term while St Kilda could manage just three points. It was all one-way traffic in the final quarter, with the crowd appreciating the last goal of the game through young defender Zach Guthrie, who had really started to find his feet in the team.

In their rivalry re-match, Sam De Koning had the better of Max King, keeping him to just one goal, while the young Cat had 11 disposals and eight intercepts. Brandan Parfitt capitalised on the absence of Selwood and Dangerfield in the middle of the ground, collecting 25 disposals, 10 clearances and six tackles, while Menegola seized his opportunity with 25 disposals and 10 score involvements. Veteran Isaac Smith kicked three goals from 21 touches to snare the three Brownlow votes, with the two votes going to Holmes, who had a career-high 24 disposals and 531 metres gained.

Up in the stands Dangerfield was smiling. He loved what Holmes brought to this team, the running ability and speed, which reminded him of an old sparring partner of his.

'There are [Chris] Judd–like traits,' Dangerfield said. 'He has phenomenal endurance but also electric speed – it's a rare combination. He hadn't played all that much footy during his junior days and I think he's just starting to find out how good he can be. We haven't played him that much as an inside mid yet, but he can be a good stoppage player as well. I believe he could be the best player in the competition at some stage, he truly could be.'

CHAPTER 22

Round 22

Saturday August 13, 4.35 pm
Metricon Stadium
Geelong 18.11.119 versus Gold Coast 9.5.59

I T'S the game that sticks in the minds of the Guthrie brothers, for a number of reasons.

The previous year in Round 20 against North Melbourne in Hobart, Zach had a breakout day, collecting a career-high 28 disposals and 13 marks. He was dominant across half-back in the Cats' 20-point win, while in the midfield Cam also had a solid afternoon with 29 touches and two goals. Both polled eight votes in the AFL Coaches' Association award, yet on Brownlow Medal night it was C Guthrie three votes, Z Guthrie zero.

'He [Zach] was furious with that,' Cam joked. 'Honestly, I think that was a really important game for Zach ... with him being on the fringe and being on one-year contracts and always feeling as if he had to prove himself. Who knows exactly, but it could have been a career-saver, showing that he can be a really important player at the level and can excel on the big stage. With the underlying repercussions, it can be a little stressful to think about as a brother when he is fighting for his career. I was very proud of him that day.'

Zach had spent most of his time at Geelong living on the edge. After being taken in the Rookie Draft in 2016 from the Calder Cannons he found a spot late into his first season.

He played nine games, including two finals, in defence and looked a prospect, but then over the next three years as his older brother was morphing into one of the Cats' best midfielders, Zach was going backwards. Eleven games in three years had his name on the whiteboard at end-of-year list management discussions. He did have one big asset in his corner, assistant coach Matthew Scarlett, who kept vouching for him.

After the North Melbourne performance, he played the next two games before going out of the side for two weeks. Importantly, he was recalled for the semi-final win over the GWS Giants and the preliminary final loss to Melbourne.

With his contract up at the end of 2022, Zach made a decision. He wasn't going to follow his brother and teammates on the regulation post-season overseas holiday.

Instead he hired an athletics coach to improve his running and body shape ahead of the biggest year of his career.

'I see what Zach does at the club every day as a teammate and I guess as a brother I have been able to experience more than that as well,' Cam said. 'He made lots of sacrifices, where in the off-season he has not gone on big trips or travelled, [he has chosen] to stay home and improve his game and hire one-on-one athletic coaches to develop himself. It is no accident he has been able to become an important player.'

But the doubts, which had been a constant throughout his previous five seasons, came back after Zach was dropped after the opening two rounds of 2022. 'I was dropped after the Sydney game [in Round 2],' he said. 'Then I was the sub for the Brisbane game. That was a challenging period for me. I was really keen to attack this season and establish myself as a player. Without playing games that were horrible [in the first two rounds], I found myself out of the team.

'The next opportunity came against GWS [in Round 8]. I wanted to make the most of that opportunity and you get to a point where you need to cash in and find yourself as part of the regulars.'

Zach had 23 disposals and kicked a goal against the Giants and hadn't looked back. That season he played every remaining game and all but one resulted in wins.

Footy was always in the Guthries' blood, not just because their father, Andrew, played VFL football for Fitzroy and Essendon under his stepfather's surname, Merryweather, before reclaiming his birth surname Guthrie. Eldest brother Ben, who is now digital manager at the AFL Players' Association, showed talent from an early age. Third son Josh played with Geelong's VFL team before returning to play football at Sunbury with Ben.

In many ways the relationship between Cam and Zach has grown at Kardinia Park given the youngest of the clan was only just preparing for high school when his brother was leaving the family home for his own AFL adventure.

Cam had been selected with the Cats' first-round pick, No.23, in the 2010 draft and made his debut in the opening game of 2011. However, he was dropped after Round 2 and never had another look-in as Geelong went on to win the premiership. 'I was on the list when the team won a premiership, but I wasn't personally involved,' he said. 'That kind of burned for a few years, even though looking back I didn't deserve to be in the team.

'I am at peace with it now, even though I would love to be involved in one. I know that I have put so much into it that I am not going to judge my career on whether I do or don't win a premiership. I feel like I have played 220-odd games of the club's last 300, so I have the runs on the board. We have so many people who put so much effort and go the extra mile to ensure the club is in a good position. It'd be nice to enjoy the end of the year with a big celebration.'

Cam has certainly come a long way since he took up a part-time job at an ice-cream shop in Geelong in his fifth year at the club. He'd decided he wanted to experience what the 'real world' was like, so once a week he was scooping ice cream at Belmont's Cold Rock.

While that employment didn't last, his day job started to take off with a breakout season in 2020, when he won the best and fairest and was selected in the All-Australian team. He followed that up in 2021, leading the Cats in disposals, averaging 29 per game; he was second in clearances, third in tackles and was the club's leading vote-getter in the Brownlow Medal, polling 18. And like his younger brother, he seemed to have elevated his game again in 2022. In the eyes of his coaches, the 30-year-old had become the best inside mid in the competition over the second half of the year.

He was coming up against a pretty good one in Gold Coast's Touk Miller in the penultimate home-and-away game, which had some extra meaning for the Guthrie boys. Zach, 24, was celebrating his 50th game in a milestone which at various times looked unlikely, but clearly his teammates were keen to embrace the moment, kicking seven goals in the opening quarter.

Leading the way was Tyson Stengle, who kicked three goals in the first quarter, which moved Hawthorn great Jason Dunstall to declare in the Fox commentary box: 'It's one of the great quarters we've seen from a small forward this year.'

At half-time the game was done with the lead out to 51 points. In the end it was 10 goals, with Jeremy Cameron enjoying roaming around Metricon Stadium, collecting 21 disposals and kicking 3.3. Mark Blicavs and Max Holmes both kicked two goals, while Miller played a lone hand for the Suns with a game-high 36 disposals.

For the Cats, it was their second-best first half of the season, their fourth-highest score and equal-third biggest winning margin of the year to date. Afterwards Chris Scott spoke about the excitement of entering his 11th finals series after his eighth top-four finish in 12 years as coach.

'But there's some anxiousness that comes with it. But you've got two choices ... you can fight that feeling [or] you can live with it and embrace it,' he said. 'It's impossible to do great things in life without that anxiety being your partner for a fair bit of it ... I'd rather risk the disappointment of not quite getting there – and it's a shocking feeling when you don't quite get there – but I'd take 100 of them to try to pull it off once.'

What he didn't mention was the rising anxiety that was starting to grip Geelong's medical team. And it had nothing to do with Rhys Stanley being subbed off for the second time in three games. Cameron had come off midway through the last quarter, many thinking it was just to keep him safe and sound, given the scoreboard. But the real story was he'd felt something in his hamstring. Given his history, and the fact the finals were three weeks away, this was a scenario that had the Cats nervous.

It was only smiles for the Guthries, who'd celebrated the family's milestone in style, Cam having 30 touches and kicking a goal while Zach was again solid across half-back with 18 disposals.

While there were no Brownlow votes for Zach – Cameron stole the three from Miller – importantly for the man of the moment there was joint love in the coaches' votes: Z Guthrie one vote, C Guthrie one vote.

CHAPTER 23

Round 23

Saturday August 20, 4.35 pm

GMHBA Stadium

Geelong 19.17.131 versus West Coast 7.4.46

JOEL Selwood popped his head into Chris Scott's office and asked if the coach had a spare minute.

The two chewing the fat was obviously a regular thing, so no-one wandering by would have had any idea of the bombshell the captain was about to drop. Scott certainly didn't.

Selwood had decided to retire at the end of the season. He'd caught up with his manager, Tom Petroro, earlier in the week and started the process.

Earlier, he'd asked Petroro to subtly sound out over the season a few of his teammates who he also managed, such as his best mates Tom Hawkins, Mitch Duncan and vice-captain Tom Stewart, to see how they thought he was travelling.

Selwood had also asked the question of Patrick Dangerfield in one of their many coffee catch-ups. They'd consistently come back with 'he could go on', which he'd expected, so on Petroro's advice it was decided he should raise the topic with Geelong CEO Steve Hocking.

'He said the same thing, it's up to me whether I go on,' Selwood explained. 'And I decided, out of all that, that I could go probably at 85 per cent next year and everyone would look after me, but I had to be all in and I just couldn't do that.'

This had all played out in the week leading up to the final game of the home-and-away season against West Coast, which fortuitously was being played at GMHBA Stadium.

Selwood thought Hocking had told Scott. He hadn't. The CEO would explain later he didn't want to ruin the special moment between captain and coach. So when Selwood started his retirement speech, Scott was blank. He had no idea what he was talking about.

'I just wanted to tell you I'm OK with the decision that I'd come to with Hock and Tommy [Petroro],' Selwood said.

Scott frowned. 'What are you talking about?'

Selwood then ran through what had happened over the past few days and within a couple of minutes two of the toughest players to have played AFL were in tears.

Scott threw a few questions at his skipper. He'd known this moment was coming eventually, although given how Selwood was playing and how the team was travelling, he wasn't expecting the conversation just now.

After a few moments, both tried to compose themselves, but then as Selwood went to walk out he turned around and again went and hugged his coach of the past 12 years. An hour later Selwood sat in the players' theatre for the team meeting. He'd managed to sort himself out, but Scott clearly hadn't.

It was Dangerfield's 300th game the following day and the coach was supposed to deliver an amazing speech talking about what the Brownlow Medallist meant to Geelong. He failed.

'Scotty probably delivered his worst performance of a pre-game speech I've ever seen, which was quite disappointing because it was Patty's 300th,' Selwood said. 'I took the moment away from him but we had a special time.'

At this stage only six people knew about the retirement.

He chose not to tell his close teammates, as he didn't want to distract their focus over the next month. He also wasn't going to tell his childhood mates or his brothers just yet, as he wanted to keep it contained while he got his head around it more himself.

The following day Selwood ran onto GMHBA Stadium for the final time and felt like a heavy weight had been lifted from his shoulders. He was happy the focus was on Dangerfield, so he could just enjoy the experience. He'd already done the acknowledgement of fans after his 350th game three weeks earlier, so all he had to do now was get about his business.

The West Coast Eagles weren't going to cause any problems, with most of the interest around the clash centring on who wasn't playing. Scans on the Monday after the Gold Coast win had shown Jeremy Cameron had suffered a low-grade strain in his right hamstring, confirming his suspicions. Despite having three separate hamstring issues last year, there was a high level of confidence he would play in the first final. It would be touch and go, but Cameron understood his body intimately given what he'd been through, and he sensed this setback was at the minor end of the scale. Rhys Stanley was also out, although his knee problem wasn't expected to put his finals campaign under any threat, while Mitch Duncan was rested. Sam Menegola was a late out, replaced by Jonathon Ceglar.

Tom Hawkins wasn't out, but he provided the funniest moment of the lead-up when he came out to run through the banner with his teammates in his warm-up T-shirt instead of playing jumper. He soon switched on and got involved in the first-half goal fest – Geelong were leading by 51 points at half-time, although they were already two men down.

Patrick Dangerfield celebrates his 300th game.

Jake Kolodjashnij had flown for a spoil on Eagle Jack Darling and landed awkwardly on his neck. He then failed a concussion test and was subbed out at quarter-time, replaced by Tom Atkins, who'd been made the medical sub only as part of a management plan of his game time.

Then in the second quarter some friendly fire ended Cam Guthrie's day. He collided with Dangerfield and in no surprise came off second best, leaving the ground clutching his shoulder. He never returned, but the initial diagnosis was positive and he sat out the game more as a precaution than anything else.

Hawkins finished with four goals to draw equal with Cameron on 59 goals, the pair tied for third in the Coleman Medal, which was won for the first time by Carlton's Charlie Curnow on 64 goals. Richmond's Tom Lynch finished second with 60. Tyson Stengle was nipping at their heels, his four-goal haul against the Eagles taking his tally to an impressive 46 goals. Dangerfield was right – Stengle did end up kicking a lot more than 35.

Selwood enjoyed his final run around GMHBA Stadium, kicking two goals from 28 disposals, while Ceglar took his opportunity again, having 24 touches and 10 clearances. Mark Blicavs, meanwhile, was best on ground with 25 disposals and 16 hit-outs.

Esava Ratugolea, who hadn't played since Round 3, produced an impressive cameo in a new role as key defender. Maybe it was a pointer to the future – a defensive partnership of the 197 cm forward and Sam De Koning in the future is an enticing prospect.

Meanwhile Dangerfield cruised through his milestone game with 22 touches in the 85-point demolition, which he described as just 'another stepping stone'.

'We understand the job at hand and what's ahead – and we can't wait for that,' he said. 'I just feel like we're ready. It's hard to compare one year to the next, but this group feels like it's ready for the challenge. I don't feel like we've peaked yet, we're still working on things and improving certain parts of our game, but it's a great group to be part of and it's a lot of fun.'

After a week off, it was now time for the finals – the time that the Cats had set themselves for all year.

CHAPTER 24

Qualifying Final

Saturday September 3, 4.35 pm
Melbourne Cricket Ground
Geelong 11.12.78 versus Collingwood 10.12.72

M ARK O'Connor was just existing.

On the surface there didn't seem to be any issues:
he was turning up each week, playing his role and the team
kept winning. But there was something wrong; his heart
wasn't in it like previous years.

'I was having a poor enough season for most of it, just
middle of the road. I lost a bit of competitive edge there
at the start of the year. I was happy to go along with the
wins,' O'Connor said. 'I felt like I wasn't pushing any
boundaries or myself for a while, to be honest. It was ... I
don't know. I just existed for a while.'

O'Connor missed the first three weeks of the season
because of a knee injury, but from then played every game

despite struggling for motivation. 'I suppose motivation was shaky early on. I was questioning everything. I think I just broke it down too much in my head,' he said.

'At the end of the day, we are kicking a bag of air through some big sticks and most of the time it is not even me kicking it. That probably hindered my motivation. I didn't know what I was doing with myself. I was probably only there for the lads at that stage, very happy to see them winning and going well. That was the whole existing thing.'

It came to a head in Round 11 against Adelaide at GMHBA Stadium, where the Cats won comfortably by 42 points but O'Connor was anything but comfortable.

'I wasn't getting involved and I didn't care, which is not like me. I remember Tom Stewart was having a stormer and I felt like I was just watching. A spectator. We were winning, it was grand, but if you are not taking pride in your own performance, you probably shouldn't be in the team,' he said.

'I remember thinking after the game, honestly if I carry on like this I shouldn't be in the team. In fairness to the coaches, they were just waiting for it to click into gear. In that game, I remember I came off with 15 minutes to go and we were going to win. I just said, "You lads can go back on. Get your possessions, get your stats." I actually sat out the rest of that game. Looking back now, that is a regret.

'At the time ... you look around and see people really changing lives, nurses and doctors, the likes. They spend their time really helping people. Saving lives, doing things like that and you wonder ... I don't know. Could you be doing something productive for people? Just the value of sport I suppose. Where I was spending my time. What I would regret and wouldn't.'

Near the end of the season he asked assistant coach James Kelly out for coffee, where he poured his heart out. The coaches knew what was happening, but had been patient hoping he would click into gear.

O'Connor suggested maybe a tagging role, which he'd done successfully previously, would give him purpose, but it didn't fit into how the team was now operating through the midfield. Instead the moment O'Connor snapped back into action came when he was named medical sub for the first time in the Round 22 game against the Gold Coast. Suddenly he had to fight for his existence, prove his worth and do it in a hurry given what was just around the corner.

It had been the first rocky episode for the 25-year-old, who was one of the best young Gaelic footballers in Ireland when he moved across the other side of the world in 2016 to play a foreign game.

After attending a draft combine in Ireland, O'Connor had been invited out to Australia by the AFL for a try-out, where he excelled in the 2-km time trial. The next day Geelong whisked him down the highway and gave him a tour of the town plus a bit of kick-to-kick, where it was obvious he had the skills required to make the transition.

The Cats had already done their research from contacts in Ireland, who spoke positively about the attitude and leadership of the Kerry minor All-Ireland winner.

He'd suffered from chronic knee problems in his last season in Ireland and the prospect of being involved in a professional club with the best medical services made it a no-brainer for O'Connor. Everything had fallen into place quickly. He debuted in his rookie year, was promoted to the leadership group in year three and then played in a Grand Final the following year.

Now, after 84 games, he was unsure of where he stood in the pecking order. He'd come back into the side against West Coast, but with some prime movers returning for the qualifying final, there was going to be some shuffling of the decks.

He wasn't the only one feeling the heat. Rhys Stanley had been dealing with a knee problem for the past month and had left the door ajar for Jonathon Ceglar, who'd impressed against the Eagles. Brandan Parfitt had come back in for the past four games and excelled, while Sam Menegola had also recovered from an injury-plagued first half of the season to put his name back in the mix.

There was one player who ignited more debate than any other at Geelong when it came to September selection – Gary Rohan. His record in finals, including some forgettable games with Sydney, didn't make for great reading, but Chris Scott decided to draw a line in the sand in relation to this predictable narrative. One of his great traits throughout his coaching career has been to always publicly back his players, no matter what the situation. If someone was attacking them, they were attacking him.

On Channel 9's *Footy Classified* in the lead-up to the qualifying final, Essendon legend Matthew Lloyd produced statistics illustrating how Rohan's form dropped off in finals compared to the regular season, including averaging just 7.9 disposals and a miserable 0.8 goals from eight finals since he joined Geelong in 2019.

He highlighted last year's preliminary final loss to Melbourne, when Rohan had just one disposal, and the 2020 grand final defeat to Richmond, when he touched the ball just five times.

Asked if he was nervous about Rohan given he was under pressure to perform, Scott said: 'I don't subscribe to that theory. I think every player is a little bit different and the art of coaching is trying to push the right buttons. Lloydy mentioned the thing we rate about him the most – there's two things. One, we think he's a great foil for [Tom] Hawkins and [Jeremy] Cameron, he's a difficult match-up if the opposition gives him too much space. And his pressure's elite.

'Having said that, I don't buy that there's pressure on him. I don't think anyone who knows footy is thinking, "for Geelong to win, Gary Rohan's got to dominate". I saw those stats. He did a hammy, he did a hammy in the prelim final. Even the numbers you put up there, they were pretty tight.

'It's a good question to ask me live on TV, because I get a bit defensive of my players, and I wear that as a badge of honour. But I think it's borderline silliness to highlight a player who none of you would have in the top 15 players in our team and say, "he's the one under the most pressure."'

After kicking 32 goals in 2021, Rohan missed the first half of 2022 with a back injury and had kicked nine goals in nine games – but the most important stat was the 26 tackles, which is what endeared him to his coach. And that's all Rohan cared about.

'He [Scott] has always stood by me, he knows the role that I play. Some people don't really see it, what effect I can have on the team,' Rohan said. 'It doesn't really bother me, you can write what you write, it doesn't bother me, I don't read it, that's your job … He has always got our backs, so the same for us – we have got his.'

The pre-finals bye gave the AFL its chance to have its awards night, on which five Cats were selected in the All-

Australian side, including Hawkins, who was named as captain. Tom Stewart received his fourth All-Australian jacket, Cameron his third, while Mark Blicavs, who had been nominated three times, finally made it into the 22. But the story of the night was clearly Tyson Stengle, the first delisted free agent to receive the honour.

Former Richmond teammate Shai Bolton, who also made his first All-Australian team, was just as excited for Stengle as he was himself.

'It's unreal. I got drafted with him,' Bolton said. 'It's probably one of the biggest stories in the AFL. I'm super proud of him and how he's played football.'

Stewart was proud to stand on the All-Australian stage with his mate, who he knew after one training session in the pre-season was very special. 'I think it was the second or third session. Tys made me look absolutely silly and I said, "Boys, we've got an absolute special one here." He turned me inside out and baulked me and kicked one over his head. I said, "I'm glad he's on our team,"' Stewart said.

'He's a special kid. He doesn't say much but we've really embraced him and the person he is and obviously, he made some mistakes in the past but he's come in and he's bought into the Geelong system, he understands how important it is for us and we love him for it.'

Scott loved the life story as much as the football side with his 23-year-old goalsneak. 'Tyson's life now compared to 12 months ago, is exponentially better and so that makes the hairs of the back of my neck stand up as much as talking about what we've got in front of us the next four weeks.'

The most pressing issue for the coach was team selection for the qualifying final against a Collingwood team who were on a similar winning streak to the Cats. While Geelong hadn't lost since Round 9, the Magpies had won 12 of their last 13 games.

Cameron had proved his fitness from the hamstring injury, while the coach's faith in Stanley stayed strong after he recovered from a knee issue. Mitch Duncan also returned after a week's rest. This meant Parfitt, who played 23 games in 2021 before cruelly missing the preliminary final because of a hamstring injury, missed out again, along with Ratugolea and Ceglar.

As for O'Connor … he was the medical sub.

It was obvious to Isaac Smith almost as soon as he walked into the rooms. Tension.

The rooms were quieter than normal, almost eerie, and it had the veteran slightly concerned.

Smith was Mr September. Tonight was his 24th AFL final since he'd burst onto the scene as a mature-aged recruit at Hawthorn back in 2011. In 12 seasons he had missed the finals only three times.

Seemingly everywhere he'd gone, and there were many destinations on his path to the big time, Smith has won premierships – at the Wagga Tigers as a kid, then with Ballarat Football League club Redan when he moved to the Victorian country town to go to university.

He started playing local footy just to meet people, starting in the reserves before winning a flag in the seniors. Midway through the following year he was invited onto North Ballarat's VFL list, where after three games in the seconds he was promoted.

Smith played in the final six games of the season, including the finals, winning the premiership and also capturing the eye of AFL scouts. Hawthorn jumped quickly to take the 21-year-old with its first pick, No.19, in the 2010 national draft. He became a regular in Alastair Clarkson's side midway through his first season and then rode the Hawks glory train, playing in four consecutive grand finals, winning three of them.

When the dynasty started to run out of steam at Hawthorn and they turned their focus to rebuilding with youth, Smith went searching for another premiership. Melbourne and Geelong both came knocking and, while the Demons' offer had more dollar signs attached, he felt the Cats were a better chance of satisfying his thirst for another flag.

While he initially got that part wrong given what Melbourne did in 2021, the move to Geelong had been great for his family, so now he had to make sure it delivered what he wanted on the football field.

The nervous energy he was sensing in the rooms wasn't going to help achieve that – players over-thinking things and picturing the game in their mind before they'd even run out was a recipe for disaster.

He sensed something needed to be said.

'Boys, come in,' Smith said to his teammates. 'There is still 20 minutes to go before the game so let's chill out a bit.'

The first final had been Geelong's biggest hurdle in finals campaigns, even worse than the preliminary finals. The stats were ugly. Since the 2011 premiership win they'd made the finals nine times and only won in the first week once. They'd lost their past six qualifying finals.

The Cats elected to start with Patrick Dangerfield and Joel Selwood on the bench for the opening bounce, which said everything about how far Tom Atkins had come. Scott wanted Atkins' defensive pressure and the bigger body of Blicavs in the middle to match up on the Magpie prime movers Jordan De Goey and Scott Pendlebury.

Collingwood's pressure was on point from the start of the game, but in a good sign for the Cats they got the first shot at goal through the man who'd been the focus of the lead-up, Rohan, but he missed a set shot from 45 metres.

From there it was all Collingwood as they got repeated inside 50s, which resulted in goals to Patrick Lipinski,

Brody Mihocek and Josh Daicos, his snap from the boundary line reminiscent of his legendary father Peter.

The Pies missed a few chances as well, and it wasn't until the 27-minute mark that Cameron opened Geelong's account with a trademark snap around the body to ensure the margin was a manageable 14 points at quarter-time.

A couple of early misses from the Pies again helped the Cats' cause before they finally settled, ramping up their own pressure, going plus 18 for contested ball in the second term. Tom Hawkins and Rohan hit the scoreboard and when Brad Close goaled on the run from long-range they led for the first time.

A goal after the siren by Pies forward Will Hoskin-Elliott wrestled back a one-point lead at the main break.

In the rooms Scott and his coaching panel were ultra positive just like they'd been all year. 'Scotty had spoken about it often, as had all the coaches, they'd said, "We are not going to get it all our own way, it is going to be a grind and embrace the grind when it eventually comes,"' Dangerfield explained. 'That had come in the first final.'

The Cats had lost the unlucky Jake Kolodjashnij after a knock on the knee, with O'Connor brought into action.

It was much of the same in the third quarter with the pressure intense, and luckily the Pies' radar was still off.

Grind. Grind. Grind.

Despite the lack of scoring no-one could take their eyes away from the game, with the biggest crowd of the season, 91,525, hanging off every contest and decision.

Eventually Collingwood youngster Ash Johnson found space and kicked the first goal of the term before Duncan replied three minutes later and then Rohan bobbed up again, charging out to mark brilliantly and convert the set shot.

An impressive snap while being tackled by Magpie midfielder Jack Crisp continued the topsy-turvy nature of the qualifying final before two miracle goals raised the excitement levels.

First it was Johnson who casually went back and kicked an incredible banana goal from the boundary line in the same MCC members' pocket where he'd kicked an identical goal a month earlier against Melbourne.

It was a Jeremy Cameron–type of goal, so a minute later the Cats superstar thought, 'I'll see you and raise you.' After Pies defender Brayden Maynard soccered the ball out of bounds on the full, Cameron lined up against the fence 45 metres out on the wrong side for a left-footer. Most thought he'd go with the banana kick but instead it was an extraordinary arrow-like drop punt, which never deviated from the middle of the goals.

The game was delivering in every pulsating minute.

A typically cool Jamie Elliott goal in the final two minutes from a set shot gave Collingwood a seven-point lead at three-quarter time.

Grind. Grind. Grind.

It was going to be a case of who blinked first in the last quarter. The Pies' matchwinner, De Goey, delivered the first strike when he got on the end of a series of handballs to kick a running goal from 30 metres in the opening minutes.

Given how close the game had been all day, a 12-point lead was a worrying gap for the Cats, who needed an answer quickly. And it was Atkins who stood up, getting the centre clearance and bombing it long, where Cameron read it better than anyone to mark at the front of the pack.

These were the moments he lived for and from 48 metres he nailed the goal. The former Giant had a hand in the Cats' next after a brilliant trap on the wing allowed Hawkins to break free and get it over to Selwood, whose pass found Stengle in space 20 metres out. He then calmly handballed over the top to Close, who ran into the open goal square to put his team back in front.

The cream was rising to the top – as it did again when De Goey put his hand up. He was putting together an incredible final term and had one more heroic act left. A clever Nick Daicos kick had released Lipinski on the wing, whose centring kick found Pendlebury. The Pies' captain then handballed to a running De Goey, who cruised to 40 metres out and nailed his second goal for the quarter.

The Pies were a goal up with five minutes left on the clock. From the subsequent centre bounce they again went forward, but Zach Tuohy stood strong at half-back to take a crucial mark. The Irishman then unloaded one of his trademark long bombs to a pack of players at centre half-forward, with all eyes in the stadium searching for the hot hand of Cameron.

But it wasn't the No.5 who split the pack open, it was that man Rohan again. 'He's marked it like Wayne Carey,' Luke Darcy screamed in Channel 7 commentary. The irony wasn't lost on anyone. The player who'd been maligned for not being able to handle finals pressure was now producing in the biggest game of the season. He went back and kicked the goal from 50 metres out.

Rohan pumped the air with his fist and roared as he was swamped by his teammates. Scores were now level with less than four minutes remaining.

Grind. Grind. Grind.

With every possession gathered like their life depended on it, players from both sides were flying all over the place. With two minutes left the ball was bouncing around Collingwood's half-forward line when Tom Stewart produced a clever kick under pressure, which Cam Guthrie marked brilliantly with one outstretched arm.

He quickly handballed to Duncan, who was immediately set on by Pendlebury, but managed to get it back to Guthrie, who looked up and kicked it wide out towards the half-forward flank, where Cameron had got a couple of metres on his opponent.

In one stride he gathered, peeked over his shoulder and saw Rohan sprinting into an empty forward 50. His kick floated high and took what felt like forever to reach Rohan, who was clearly thinking that as he dropped a straightforward chest mark.

Luckily for him Collingwood's Steele Sidebottom slipped over, which allowed him to stagger after the bouncing ball and then to his great delight he looked up to see Max Holmes all by himself at the top of the goal square. Rohan finally got hold of the bobbling Sherrin and gave it off to the youngster, who sent it into the stands. The Cats were six points up with 83 seconds left.

Like a well-oiled machine Geelong did everything right in the final minute to ensure Collingwood didn't get the chance for a Hail Mary. Fittingly the final act of the game was Rohan desperately diving at Magpies defender Isaac Quaynor to put pressure on his kick into the forward line. The matchwinner was on his back when the siren sounded and he soon had Cameron on top of him.

'One of the great games of footy I have ever seen,'

Demons great Garry Lyon said on Fox Footy. No-one would argue with him.

What was immediately obvious straightaway was the relief on the faces of the Geelong players, and their love for Gary Rohan. He finished with three goals, 14 disposals, four marks and two tackles to put to bed the narrative about his inability to perform in September.

'We're just so proud of him,' Isaac Smith said. 'We've got a great group ... but he was unbelievable today and he won us the game.'

Smith added that, while he didn't know how Rohan had absorbed the criticism, 'It's impossible not to hear it these days with phones and technology. You can't hide under a rock.'

Tuohy was happy Rohan would now get the recognition he deserved. 'Gaz brings incredibly consistent effort and output, he doesn't always get the reward on the stats sheet,' Tuohy said. 'But it was nice for him to get the reward tonight because some of the stuff he does is just unbelievable and he rarely gets the recognition externally for it. He'll get the recognition internally as he always does, but it's nice that everyone on the outside gets to see it as well.'

Scott was glowing afterwards about his match-winning forward's performance. 'It is gratifying, I don't mind saying that. We are really clear on what he can bring to our team and the way we play. He's absolutely an energy giver, his teammates love playing with him and I'm just really proud of him.'

While Rohan deservedly captured all the headlines there were warrior-like efforts by others in the blue and white hoops. Cameron was supreme with three goals from 17 touches, Atkins had 23 disposals and nine tackles, while Selwood had thrived on the occasion with 25 inspired touches.

Later that night back at home in Barwon Heads, the skipper was still taking in the enormity of the qualifying final when his wife, Brit, brought up retirement. He figured she was about to suggest holiday locations, but instead she wanted to talk footy. He'd been one of the best players in Geelong's last two games, and he was fitter and healthier than she'd ever seen him before at this time of the year.

'Are we making the right decision?'

CHAPTER 25

Preliminary Final

Friday September 16, 7.50 pm
Melbourne Cricket Ground
Geelong 18.12.120 versus Brisbane 7.7.49

PATRICK Dangerfield is always searching, looking, enquiring, asking. He constantly wants to know more about life. Things that wouldn't be on the radar of most footballers intrigue him.

The Brownlow Medallist is unique in many ways, and as he entered another finals series and another opportunity to win the elusive premiership, the power of the mind was becoming a fascination.

He'd heard all the noise around his own performances in finals, how there was a perception that he tried too hard to do everything, be the man, be the star who carried the team to the promised land. Maybe he had been guilty of that in the past, but now at the age of 32 he was more reflective. He'd already come to the realisation that a premiership – or the lack of one – wouldn't define him.

'I remember listening to [Fremantle captain] Matthew Pavlich, and this was maybe 2016, and he was at a grand final," Dangerfield said. 'He was talking about, and I'm paraphrasing here, he was talking about satisfaction, and still feeling complete, even though he hadn't won it [the premiership].

'I didn't quite get it at the time, like, you haven't won it, how could you feel complete when you've had this incredible career, just how could you feel complete. But I get it now, having not won one. Footy for me has provided so much. I will always be, and Mards [wife Mardi] as well, we will be so grateful for football, honestly. Words can't describe how grateful we are and what it's provided for our family and me.

'So, it's perhaps with that more balanced wisdom of life and its experiences that you can acknowledge that, hell yeah, a premiership is all that matters now and nothing else scratches that itch. But if it doesn't happen, it's actually not the end of the world. For some people, they will find that preposterous.'

Now that he was neck-deep again in the hunt for a premiership, Dangerfield went searching for more understanding. He found a podcast called *Finding Mastery*. It was produced by high-performance psychologist Dr

Michael Gervais, who'd worked closely with NFL team the Seattle Seahawks and their Super Bowl–winning coach Pete Carroll.

Throughout his career Gervais had followed a central question: 'Is there a common thread connecting how the greatest performers in the world use their minds to pursue the boundaries of human potential?' He'd worked with business leaders, artists, musicians and sportspeople at the highest level, training their mindset skills and practices.

Dangerfield was interested, so he reached out to Gervais and arranged to spend time with him in the lead-up to the preliminary final. They chatted for hours on Zoom and the Cats superstar came away convinced he was a better person for the experience.

'He talks about the moment and not building it up to be any bigger than what it actually is,' Dangerfield said. 'At the end of the day, it's another moment. He's a US guy and spending time and chatting with him was brilliant. Not that you view the game differently, but you view it as just another moment. So, you understand what it is, and we understand as a team and individually it's a game we want to win, but it's just another game.

'So, it sort of grounds what can be perceived and built up to something enormous, but it's something we've done so many times right throughout the year, so it's sort of connected for me.'

While Dangerfield was finding his zen, concern was growing about the state of one of Geelong's other veteran stars.

Tom Hawkins had developed soreness in his foot over the last month of the season, which had significantly reduced his ability to train during the week. It was most likely that he'd require surgery at the end of the season, but the Cats' medicos were confident they could get him to the line for two more games. Hawkins would hardly train in the lead-up to the preliminary final after the doctors issued an edict to 'keep him off his feet'.

He had company in the rehab group. Jake Kolodjashnij must have been wondering why he'd had such bad luck given the circumstances that had conspired to dramatically limit his playing time over the past month.

The defender was concussed in the first quarter of the final home-and-away game against West Coast. The week's break before the finals meant he could play in the qualifying final, but he was subbed out again early with a knee issue. Their win meant the Cats now had another week without a game, and he needed that week to recover from the knock on the knee. That's not a lot of football or training at the wrong end of the season, which was a point of discussion as the coaching panel looked ahead to taking on Brisbane at the MCG in the preliminary final.

It had been an intriguing finals series, with reigning premier Melbourne suffering a shock loss to the Lions in the previous week's semi-final at the MCG. Brisbane had survived a scare in the elimination final at home against Richmond, scraping home by two points after a freak Joe Daniher goal in the dying minutes.

The surprise had been the straight sets exit of the Demons, who'd been upstaged by the Sydney Swans in the qualifying final, which had turned the finals series on its head. Collingwood had then bounced back from its epic loss to Geelong, easily handling the Fremantle Dockers in the semi-final to set up a preliminary final showdown with the Swans at the SCG.

For James Kelly, the mood of the players had changed dramatically after they'd survived the scare against the Pies. History showed there was always a nervous finals game thrown in somewhere during the campaign. He'd played in a couple, including a memorable preliminary final win over Collingwood by just five points in 2007. The following week the Cats played with a sense of freedom, resulting in a record-breaking grand final victory over Port Adelaide to the tune of 119 points.

Kelly sensed something similar was happening in 2022. The scare had been put to bed and the training over the week off had been eye-opening. 'The conversations on the Monday, Tuesday, Wednesday after the Collingwood game were about how good it was that we played that way and still won,' the Cats assistant coach said.

'We have now got time to breathe, enjoy the week and train. All year they had trained their arses off and the week of the prelim, they were going hammer and tongs, bashing each other at training, which was amazing.'

The coaches had looked back at vision of the clash with Brisbane earlier in the year in Round 4 and one thing that stood out was how different Sam De Koning looked. 'We were saying that was back before DK was DK, that was when DK was still just Sam,' Kelly said.

A lot of the planning for Brisbane was again around Brownlow Medallist Lachie Neale, who had been amazing in the first final against Richmond, carrying his team on his shoulders with an incredible 39 disposals. The Cats had previously used Mark O'Connor as a dedicated tag on Neale with some success, but assistant coach Shaun Grigg was bullish that a committee approach was the better option.

Chris Scott was keeping the Lions guessing when quizzed in the lead-up. 'He's [Neale's] had a great season and I'd expected he'd win the Brownlow,' the Cats coach said. 'In the last two weeks he's been terrific as well, so he needs to get some attention. It's kind of Russian roulette if you try to play too offensively against him. As always with us, it's a collective and it can be a little deceiving to see the match-ups at the first bounce, because it could well be very different five or six minutes later.'

Come game time, there was one very significant change at the first bounce – Dangerfield was back in the middle and Tom Atkins started on the interchange next to Joel Selwood, who was celebrating yet another career milestone. The Cats' skipper had joined Hawthorn great Michael Tuck, who played 426 games over 20 seasons including seven flags, for most finals played – 39, which left a tantalising piece of history for the following week, not that Selwood needed any extra motivation. He was already on his own personal crusade.

Neale got the first clearance of the game only for Max Holmes to take a mark on the wing and then drive the ball to centre half-forward, where Geelong's star midfielder Patrick Dangerfield took a courageous mark running back with the flight. While some have pointed to his goalkicking as the one slight negative in his game, there were no problems with Dangerfield's perfectly struck set shot from 45 metres.

The Lions got the next goal through former Cat Lincoln McCarthy, but the signs were already positive as the game was being played on Geelong's terms. They were manufacturing a loose player behind the ball in Tom Stewart as the Lions pushed an extra up into the contest, which was captain Dayne Zorko, who'd started at half-forward.

It was the ideal scenario for Geelong.

A great tackle by Tyson Stengle on Lions defender Brandon Starcevich was rewarded with a holding the ball free kick, which resulted in the Cats' second goal of the night, before Dangerfield stamped himself on the contest again. It came after a wonderful Cam Guthrie tap with Dangerfield drilling the 45-metre goal off one step. Brisbane responded through a set shot from Callum Ah Chee before Holmes converted a free kick on the siren to give the Cats a 14-point lead at the first break.

There was a freedom about the way Geelong were playing compared to two weeks ago. Scott could sense it and so could the players. That translated into a commanding second quarter where the Cats kicked the final three goals. The first of the sequence summed up the night for the Lions' tall forwards, who were hardly sighted.

Eric Hipwood, who'd been the star against Melbourne a week earlier with four goals, hadn't got near it, and when he dropped a simple chest mark on the wing Zach Guthrie pounced, driving the ball to Gary Rohan in the forward pocket, who goaled. Tom Hawkins actually fell over while setting up a shot for goal, but still managed to get a handball to Jeremy Cameron, who handballed to Gryan Miers who slotted it. Hawkins found the middle of the sticks with a snap from close range after a series of handballs from Miers and Holmes found him alone in the forward pocket.

Hawkins had found the spotlight on him for the wrong reasons in the first half, with his normally reliable radar completely off. The full-forward missing a set shot directly in front from 25 metres. At half-time he'd kicked 1.3. The Cats' lead was 30 points but clearly could have been a lot more given their dominance.

The committee approach to Neale had been a big win with Atkins, Selwood and Guthrie taking their turns to physically clamp down on the Lions' star at every stoppage. It was brilliantly executed, with the Brownlow Medal favourite touching the ball only once in the first 20 minutes of the second quarter. It was the same for the Lions' other gun midfielder, Hugh McCluggage, who was also limited to one disposal as the Cats flexed their muscles.

Any hope of a Lions rear-guard action after the main break were quickly put to bed with a Stengle special, a snap over his shoulder from the boundary 40 metres out, and Jeremy Cameron's first for the evening after a free kick.

Three minutes later a brilliant Miers pass gave Hawkins the opportunity to exorcise his goalkicking demons. Despite this being the hardest shot of them all, from 40 metres out deep into the forward pocket, he produced his trademark left-to-right fade on the drop punt, which sailed straight through.

The dam wall was breaking.

A typical Selwood clearance set up the next, with the skipper's handball finding Brad Close, who then flicked it to Rohan for his second of the preliminary final. Everything they touched was turning to gold ... until Holmes went on another of his searching runs along the Shane Warne Stand wing. Again he'd been influential, but it was his 12th possession that dramatically changed the narrative of the night for the Cats.

The young star went to kick inboard to Isaac Smith and just as the ball left his boot, shooting pain went through his right leg. He knew straightaway something was seriously wrong, and so did the 77,677 fans inside the MCG. Holmes pulled up straightaway and raised his arm to the interchange bench. As he hobbled off, the Cats coaches' box fell silent. Despite playing only his 30th game, the kid had become such an important cog in the way the Cats played.

The television cameras caught Holmes punching the ground in frustration as he lay in front of the bench while the medical staff assessed his leg. Reality was quickly sinking in – the Cats were going to play in the grand final and he wasn't going to be in it. Or so he thought.

That's what Scott was feeling when he left the box early to get down to the bench to comfort Holmes. But when he got downstairs the doom and gloom he was expecting wasn't there. The medical team were confident it wasn't a tear and were working on the theory it was a spasm, which meant there was hope. They would need to do a scan, but there was genuine optimism that Holmes wasn't done.

Scott was surprised and relieved as he walked out to the three-quarter time huddle with the scoreboard showing his team was now 63 points up. They'd just kicked seven goals in the third term in a brutal takedown of the Lions.

The ball movement had been sublime at times and there was one player who seemed to be in almost every passage. In many ways he was an unlikely hero, but Gryan Miers was playing the game of his career. His role, along with Close's, was critical to how Geelong operated. They were the connectors, working up and down the ground, helping out the defenders, linking up with the midfield and then doing their thing in the forward line.

They blew up the GPS, clocking 15-plus kilometres most games, some of that unrewarded running where they'd work to cover a teammate's opponent. And while they worked up the ground, it allowed Stengle to stay deep as the designated goalsneak, feeding off Hawkins and Cameron and doing what he was best at – kicking goals.

Miers, playing his 82nd game, got involved in the scoring too, kicking his second of the night in the third quarter. His ability to kick goals as a junior had caught the club's eye. He was drafted by the Cats in the fourth round of the 2017 National Draft after kicking seven goals for the Geelong Falcons in the TAC Cup grand final. The 179 cm goalsneak from Torquay was the Falcons' leading target for the season, kicking more than 50 goals to put his name up in lights for recruiters.

And what about his name? How did parents Dave and Kerry come up with it?

'I think they had a Scrabble board out and they were just seeing what looked cool and what they liked,' Miers said. 'They liked "Ryan" but they wanted a bit more creativeness in it, so they added the "G" and went with that. It's been pretty annoying because no-one could say it when they'd first meet me, but I've got used to it. I don't know anyone else in the world called Gryan, so at least it's myself.' According to the AFL records, he is the first player in the competition's history to have the first name Gryan.

There is certainly a creative streak in the family, with Dave inventing the Blade football boots – initially just for himself, before turning it into a successful business, which he sold just before Gryan was born.

Adding further to Miers' quirkiness is the kicking style, which has the purists up in arms given he always veers out to the right and kicks across his body for field kicking and set shots. It looks wrong, according to the manual it is wrong, yet it works for Miers, which he showed with great pleasure with his second goal of the preliminary final at the 20-minute mark of the third quarter.

His magical night continued at the start of the final term as he found the leading Cameron with a beautiful pass, duly converted into his second goal of the game.

That drew him level with Hawkins for the season on 63 goals, but that changed again two minutes later after Dangerfield, who was clearly best on ground, went long to a one-on-one between the Tomahawk and Harris Andrews. The ball spilled over the back. Hawkins was the quickest to recovery, easily rolling through his fourth for the night from the angle.

Potentially Geelong's greatest moment of the preliminary final – or at least the best example of what they'd become – came at the eight-minute mark.

Tom Stewart played on from full-back and kicked long to a contest on the wing, where the Sherrin slipped through the fingers of Mark Blicavs into the arms of Close at the back of the pack. He quickly handballed to Miers, who had Isaac Smith running on his outside. Another quick handball brought Mitch Duncan in and by this stage Close had sprinted forward and got himself in position to get the ball back. He then ran unchecked to the 40-metre mark and kicked the goal of the night. It was a training drill.

And in a nice piece of theatre, the honour for the final goal went to Zach Guthrie, one of the faces of the new Geelong. He intercepted a sloppy Brisbane attempted pass at centre half-forward, went back and kicked the sixth goal of his career from 45 metres out.

The final margin was 71 points. Brisbane had been restricted to just seven goals for the night which illustrated how well the Cats' defence played. In the previous two finals the Lions had kicked 14 and 16 goals respectively.

In keeping with the theme of unlikely heroes, Geelong's best defender had been the one who nearly didn't play. Jake Kolodjashnij had moved better than he ever had, shrugging off concerns about his knee to collect a career-high 23 disposals, including nine marks.

Like Miers, he picked a great time to play the best game of his life. While he wasn't quite in the Rohan or Rhys Stanley league for derision by Cats fans, there had been times during his 154-game career where questions had been asked. But Scott had been in the Kolodjashnij camp for a long time, given the 193 cm defender's ability to play on smalls and talls.

Since arriving from Launceston in the 2013 National Draft at pick No.41 – his twin brother Kade went at No.5 to the Gold Coast – Kolodjashnij had been a slow burn, and after his late-season injury issues there was a suggestion his spot was under review. However, his coach moved quickly to rule out any nervousness, telling the 27-year-old that if he was fit, he played. That shot of confidence had clearly done the job, launching his starring role in a performance that had the football world predicting big things in eight days' time.

'They are a different group, they are a different looking group,' Saints champion Nick Riewoldt told Fox Footy. 'The personnel is different and the game style is different. It was built for now, it was built for tonight and for next week. I thought we got a great snapshot of what it looked like tonight with Geelong. Their ability to take the footy from one end of the ground to the other was breathtaking at times, the class divide was enormous. They are just so far and away a better team.'

CHAPTER 26

Grand Final Week

THE crowd rose to their feet as one. Max Holmes had appeared at the top of the players' race at GMHBA Stadium.

With each step the noise got louder and, by the time he'd jogged 15 metres, the thousands of fans who were at the Cats' Monday open training session were clapping their hands in unison. It was the type of reception usually reserved for a player who'd just kicked a crucial goal and was coming off to the interchange bench.

Holmes jogged a lap as his teammates watched with interest. They were as shocked as everyone else given they'd feared the worst on Friday night. He was moving smoothly and clearly the occasion got to him as he kept going for a second lap.

The scans had come back all good – there was no significant damage to the hamstring. The theory was the pain he had suffered was a neurological issue, which may have stemmed from Holmes suffering a knock to his lower back during the game. His range of movement had come back quickly and the Geelong doctors were confident he would be able to prove his fitness by Friday.

After their Friday night win, the players had been given the weekend off, and had all watched the broadcast of Sydney defeating Collingwood in a dramatic second preliminary final at the SCG. After leading by 30 points at half-time, the Swans had stopped to a walk in the last quarter as the Magpies surged, kicking the last three goals of the game to get within one point.

It had been a gripping contest and straightaway the debate about what was the best path to the Grand Final had been ignited – the hard-fought emotional contest or a free-flowing perfectly executed game. The Cats were more than happy to have won so convincingly, given they'd already had their nail-biter in the first week of the finals. They had had their doubt, followed by a confidence booster.

Tom Atkins had been more invested than most in Sydney's win; he'd been good family friends with the McCartney brothers, Paddy and Tom, since childhood. Paddy, the former No.1 draft pick at St Kilda, who had fought back from career-threatening concussion issues, was one of the stories of the Grand Final. He'd quickly slid into the WhatsApp group he shared with Atkins after the preliminary final.

'There is a group of us blokes, close mates, and he messaged not long after the game said, "Alright who are you going for?"' Atkins said. 'That was pretty funny. We have been in contact the whole finals series really. He's been really supportive of me, so it's great.

'It's a bit surreal that we get to play in a Grand Final against each other. It is nothing that we could have imagined when we were going to our Christmas parties with each other when we were 12 years old. I am super proud of him the way he has played this year, and Tommy as well, they are going so well.'

Geelong had its own brothers storyline, with Cam and Zach Guthrie joining some illustrious company. Gary and Nathan Ablett won a premiership together in 2007; twins Alistair and Stewart Lord played in the 1963 flag while Les and Peter Hardiman were together in two Cats premierships, 1931 and 1937. And coach Chris Scott had played in two premierships with his twin, Brad, at Brisbane.

There was another odd little crossover storyline: the opposing ruckmen had once been teammates, both Rhys Stanley and Sydney ruckman Tom Hickey playing with the Saints in 2013 and 14.

'I love playing against Tommy, he is a great guy and we have a great relationship,' Stanley said. 'There is always a good bit of banter on the field which is good fun. We had two or three years together at St Kilda and built a great relationship. We still have a bunch of mutual mates that are already flicking through the banter which is fun. He [Hickey] has got some tricks, he's got some stuff you have to be careful of, so it will be a good battle.'

Gary Rohan grew up a mad Sydney fan on a dairy farm in Cobden, in south-west Victoria, and then went on to play 106 games with the Swans after being taken at No.6 in the 2009 draft. He also played in two losing Grand Finals in the red and white. 'I have always followed Sydney and always barracked for them and I was actually barracking for them on the weekend,' Rohan said. 'I'm quite excited to go up against the Swans.'

The Jed Bews story was one that tugged at the heartstrings of Cats fans given his father, Andrew, had been a favourite son – tough, uncompromising and as hard as they come. He'd been one of Geelong's best players in the hallowed 1989 Grand Final against Hawthorn. He then missed the 1992 Grand Final because of injury before finishing his 282-game career at Brisbane, where he played with the Scott brothers.

Andrew returned to live in Geelong and reconnected with the club as a runner for a few years, with his youngest son always hanging around the rooms dreaming of wearing the blue and white hoops. When it came to decision-time about his football, the pull of athletics was strong given Jed was an elite junior pole-vaulter, potentially Australia's next Steve Hooker.

Football, though, won out and Jed was drafted as a father-son selection, No.86, in the 2011 draft. He took a while to find his feet. 'He was a runt when he went down there,' Andrew said. 'He didn't play a game for two years. Jed's excelled, it's just taken time. I say to people, "Jed's been a 10-year overnight success."'

Now a crucial part of the Cats' much-vaunted defence, Jed, 28, understands what it would mean to his family if he could do what his father couldn't. 'It is pretty obvious with the '89 Grand Final how it went and how close my old boy got to a flag,' he says. 'He didn't quite get there, so I would love to win a flag and it would be partly for him and for the rest of my family. To share that success with them would be awesome, so it is definitely a little bit for him and a little bit for me.'

Jed was on the couch with his dad – he was back staying at the family home while he built a new house – for the traditional Monday night Brownlow Medal count, where his teammates were on the waters and segregated off in a room away from the main ballroom at Crown Casino as a Covid precaution.

The highlight of the night was when the Channel 7 cameras caught Jeremy Cameron eating watermelon as he got another best-on-ground. The key forward polled 19 votes – 10 behind the winner, Carlton's Patrick Cripps – to be the Cats' leading vote-getter, ahead of Cam Guthrie on 13, with Tom Stewart and Mark Blicavs tied on nine votes.

Isaac Smith polled five votes, but the league's fairest-and-best night was the furthest thing from his mind. It had been a tough week for him, and behind the laid-back personality and trademark grin he was hiding some personal pain. Before the preliminary final Smith had driven to Albury to see his granddad. Kevin Smith had fallen suddenly ill, and his grandson dashed to spend 24 hours by his bedside.

'That's probably why I didn't get a touch for the first half [against Brisbane],' Smith said. 'He had a lot to do with the person I am today. I raced up there just before the prelim final and got to spend 24 hours with him, which was nice. And I'll be forever grateful that he was still mentally there and we had a great 24 hours together. He was a great man. He was my hero growing up, then he was my role model when I became a young man.'

On the Wednesday of Grand Final week, Kevin, 93, passed. His death had come quickly and taken the family by surprise. 'He was just such a humble, cheeky, well-mannered gentleman, so I feel honoured to have him as a grandfather,' Smith said. Kevin had loved watching him on the last Saturday in September when he was at Hawthorn, so Isaac was intent on celebrating that memory when he did it as a Cat in three days' time.

Smith's fellow wingman, Max Holmes, was doing his best to control his emotions as he faced the biggest few days of his life. Holmes hadn't trained at the Cats' main session, but he was continuing to impress the medical team with the movement in his leg and running. As far as the medicos were concerned, everything was on track. While the coaches were hopeful, the reality was they had to start planning around him not being there. Playing injured players in Grand Finals was frowned upon, although Scott would have remembered the example of his Brisbane teammate Nigel Lappin, who was among the best in the 2003 Grand Final despite playing with two broken ribs and a punctured lung.

The dilemma was who to replace him with if he didn't come up physically. Brandan Parfitt was clearly the best player outside of the 22 – but he was an inside midfielder, whereas Holmes' strength was his running on the outside. Mark O'Connor, who had been medical sub for the two finals, had a big engine, so physically he was better suited in that part of the equation. And then there was Sam Menegola, a pure wingman, but he'd been in and out of the side after an injury-interrupted start to the season. Do you go for the best player (Parfitt) or the more versatile option (O'Connor)? Or do you trust the veteran (Menegola) despite limited exposure?

Sydney were dealing with their own injury issues. Flexible tall forward Sam Reid had injured his quad in the preliminary final. He'd had an excellent second half of the season, working well as a foil for Lance Franklin, as well as helping out Hickey in the ruck.

When the Grand Final teams were submitted on Thursday afternoon both Holmes and Reid were named – and the Swans had made an interesting move. They had dropped young forward Logan McDonald in favour of Hayden McLean, a traditional back-up ruckman, who hadn't played since Round 8. It told the Cats that they were worried Reid wouldn't be able to do his regular ruck work and that they were gambling on him as a forward only.

D-day for Holmes was Friday morning. All week he'd ticked every box the medical and conditioning staff had put in front of him.

There was no dint to that confidence during the intense secret session at GMHBA Stadium, in which Holmes ran and kicked with freedom. He headed up to Melbourne for the Grand Final Parade believing his miracle comeback was on track.

For the first time players would not be driven through the streets of the CBD for the parade. Instead, the players were going to be on boats floating down the Yarra River. It was a risky play – and it didn't quite land. The fans simply weren't close enough to the players, who for the most part appeared bemused by the whole exercise.

There was no joking at the Grand Final press conference though, where the focus was on both clubs' injured players.

Scott was asked about Holmes. 'He's probably done what he's needed to do from a physical point of view. We were hoping we'd be at the point now where we could absolutely say that he was playing. What we do know is that it's absolutely not a "no". We just need to make sure that we spend the requisite time over the next little bit working through whether he's absolutely right and whether that's the best thing for us. We haven't absolutely made that decision just yet.'

Joel Selwood batted off retirement questions as he focused on his record-breaking 40th finals appearance. 'Another one trying to push me out the door,' Selwood laughed. 'I just feel so lucky that I've been able to be in a good side along the journey ... 40 finals, it's probably crept up on me. Right from the outset, I've played among a lot of good players. I play every game like it's my last. This one will be the same.'

Selwood had one little favour he wanted to do for his good friend Gary Ablett Jnr. Selwood had contacted his former teammate, and his wife, Jordan, during the week, and asked if he could run through the banner at the Grand Final with their son Levi. They'd been public about Levi's battle with a rare and degenerative disease, and Selwood was keen to put a smile on their faces.

'I think it's only fair that an Ablett is performing on Grand Final day, and it's Gazza's turn to cheer on his little son,' Selwood said. 'That will be pretty special for the Ablett family, but also the Geelong faithful.'

Selwood enjoyed having a moment during the leisurely captain's run at the MCG, where the Cats players had a light jog and bit of kick-to-kick. It was the second last time he'd be in the middle of the iconic stadium and he had a good vibe about it all.

By contrast Holmes was trying to keep up a positive vibe. He'd remained in his tracksuit while his teammates stretched their legs, given he'd trained earlier, and he was still in the dark when he returned to the team hotel.

Then he got the message. The coach wanted to see him in his room.

The meeting lasted less than a minute. He was out. His Grand Final dream was over.

For Scott, the risk was too high. He would later describe the call as 'brutal'. There were too many what if's. What if a player was concussed and then Holmes' hamstring went? They would then be two players down in the biggest game of the year.

A shattered Holmes retreated to his room. Down the hallway O'Connor was getting the call with good news for him – he was in the team. There were mixed feelings. One of his best mates at the club was Parfitt – and the pair had made a pledge to tell each other straightaway if they found out what was happening. At the very least they wanted to be in the 23 together, because the medical sub also received a premiership medal.

They were going to get their wish. Parfitt was now the medical sub.

'When I found out, he was in a hotel room across the hall from me,' O'Connor said. 'I didn't know if he knew. We had both made promises to each other that if one of us found out we'd tell the other. Anyway, I got the call. I just walked across the hall and gave him a big hug. See, only the 23 who are named for the final get a medal, no-one else on the list does, which is a disgrace in my opinion. It was emotional when I went across to him. He was one of the lads who came to Dingle [in Ireland] a couple of years ago with me and we're very close.'

Word about Holmes didn't leak out until 9 am the following morning. By this stage TV cameras were staking out the Cats' hotel in Albert Park, with Scott pictured going for his morning run and Selwood taking a stroll with his wife, Britt.

The players went about their own business in the morning – some had elected to return to home to sleep in their own beds back in Geelong – before making their way to the MCG by around midday.

Smith had been through the scenario plenty of times and was feeling chilled when he got into the hotel lift to go down to the lobby. Twenty seconds later he wasn't feeling chilled. The lift had stopped and the doors wouldn't open.

Things started to get serious when contact was made with the technician, who said he was an hour away. ‹I thought "oh, shit, I might not make it,"' Smith said. Fifteen minutes later, out of the blue, the doors opened. Smith was free but he couldn't help but wonder if the lift episode was a sign of how his day was going to play out.

CHAPTER 27

2022 AFL Grand Final

Saturday September 24, 2.30 pm

Melbourne Cricket Ground

Geelong 20.13.133 versus Sydney 8.4.52

THERE were no props or inspirational quotes on the whiteboard.

Chris Scott had been consistent in his messaging all season and he wasn't about to change in the hour before the Grand Final. Scott had constantly talked about what his team had to do to get their game style going. He was always asking, 'How do we get it better? How do we keep improving? How do we play better?'

He never spoke about winning. It was always about what can be done so the players can execute the game plan properly. The Cats' coach knew if they did that, no-one could stop them.

So as Robbie Williams was wowing the 100,024 fans outside on the ground, Scott was keeping to his script in the pre-game meeting. 'We have got one more chance to get our game going as well as we can,' he said.

Then Isaac Smith again addressed the group like he had before the qualifying final against Collingwood. 'Boys, let's remember we need to be ready at the start of the game, we don't need to be ready 20 minutes before the game,' he said.

There was a confidence and steely resolve about the Geelong players as they walked up the race.

The sun was beaming down and the MCG was picture perfect when Joel Selwood emerged first and walked over to Gary Ablett. The pair had a quick hug as Levi was passed over to the Geelong captain. He held the boy to his chest and as they ran through the banner Levi's smile melted the hearts of millions watching around the country. The former teammates again embraced as Levi went back into his father's arms and Selwood gave his mate's famous bald head a rub for good luck.

Next to them was Zach Tuohy, who was also sharing a special moment. It was the Irishman's 250th game and he had his two boys, Rafferty and Flynn, with him as he walked through the banner. He'd already had a few pinch-me moments in the lead-up. The premiership obsession was about to be fulfilled.

FIRST QUARTER

The first kick of the grand final was Dangerfield's.

It was fitting given how far away from that moment he'd been at times throughout the year, and even just three weeks earlier he wasn't in at the centre bounce for the first final. His kick scrubbed forward and then bobbled around as Rhys Stanley followed it up and got a handball towards centre half-forward. There were players everywhere before Sydney's goalsneak Tom Papley, who'd started in the centre square, got a quick clearing kick to the wing.

Tuohy beat Isaac Heeney to the bouncing ball and then delivered the first clear kick of the grand final to a leading Tom Hawkins, who marked close to the boundary right next to the 50-metre line. As he lined up for his shot at goal, which ended up staying too far right for a behind, there was a lot of chatter in the Geelong coaches' box about how the Swans had set up.

There weren't too many surprises. As expected, tagger Ryan Clarke had gone to Tom Stewart to play as a defensive forward, while Robbie Fox had gone to Jeremy Cameron with Tom McCartin on Hawkins.

At the other end Jack Henry was on Lance Franklin with Sam De Koning taking Sam Reid.

The one unknown for the Cats' coaching group was actually about some of their own. During the week Scott had spoken with Tuohy, Isaac Smith and Mitch Duncan about how they would set up if Holmes didn't get up.

There was some specific positioning about how he wanted them to set up, but who did what and what rotations they did was left to the players to sort out. This was the 2022 version of Scott at its best – he was guiding the players, not over-coaching and, importantly, giving them ownership. They were three of his most experienced players and he trusted them to come up with a plan, which started with Smith on the wing, Duncan at half-forward and Tuohy across half-back.

After Sydney won four of the first five clearances of the game, Geelong settled. They dominated the first 10 minutes, with the contested possession count 12-6 and inside-50s 6-1.

There is a well-worn coaching philosophy, 'don't get beaten by what you know'. John Longmire must have been pulling out his hair after watching Hawkins do a number on Tom Hickey – twice. The Cats' full-forward is renowned for his expertise at boundary line throw-ins around goal, where he out-muscles his opponent, takes possession and then gets a shot away at goal. At the 10-minute mark he did just that, easing Hickey under the ball and then snapping the goal over his shoulder. Five minutes later in the other forward pocket, he did it again with a clever banana kick.

Will Hayward got the Swans' first goal a minute later with an opportunistic snap after roving the pack 30 metres out, before the Cats made a statement. A long ball from Dangerfield was marked by Mark Blicavs in the forward pocket, who converted the set shot. Then Smith, with black tape around his left bicep in honour of his grandfather, kicked consecutive running goals to blow the Grand Final open.

There were already plenty of heroic acts from players wearing the blue and white hoops. Dangerfield was throwing himself into contests while Mark O'Connor had started on the wing with a rundown tackle on Sydney's James Rowbottom, his first statement in the game.

Smith had a hand in the Cats' final goal of the quarter, his quick kick finding Brad Close, who nailed the set shot from 40 metres out in the pocket.

The siren couldn't come quick enough for Sydney – Geelong's 6.5.41 its highest score ever in the opening quarter of a Grand Final. It was also the highest score Sydney had conceded for the season. The 113-67 possession count lead was the fourth-highest margin in any game for the year.

And the two most influential players on the ground? They were the two oldies whose whole season had been aimed at peaking on this day via management programs and a disciplined long-term plan. Selwood, who had started on the bench, led all comers with 12 disposals, while Dangerfield had been inspiring with six possessions – five of which were contested – and three clearances.

SECOND QUARTER

Tyson Stengle wrote his name into the Geelong record books when he launched a set shot from 50 metres to convert his 50th goal of the season at the four-minute mark. For the first time in the club's history, three players – Hawkins, Cameron and Stengle – had topped the 50-goal mark.

The stats sheet was flashing red lights everywhere for the Swans as the Cats clocked up 19 inside-50s to two in between Sydney's first two goals. Hayden McLean posted their second with a one-handed mark in the goal square at the eight-minute mark.

By midway through the quarter there was movement in the Geelong coaches' box, as there were signs Sydney was getting its game going. They'd only had 16 handball receives in the first quarter yet at the 12-minute mark of the second they'd already had 15. The Swans were trying to possess the ball with short kicks and overlapping run and handball. The message was sent down to Cats runner Shannon Byrnes to tell the leaders: 'Don't let them mark it.' There needed to be more emphasis on limiting the easy marks.

A free kick to Hawkins in a one-on-one contest with Tom McCartin saw him kick his third, which equalled his best in a grand final and extended the lead to 42 points.

Sydney co-captain Callum Mills replied shortly after, but then another Dangerfield clearance to Tom Atkins resulted in a pass to Stengle on the lead, who nailed his second long-range shot for the day.

Just before half-time Heeney, who had been well held by Jake Kolodjashnij, managed to get free, kicking a goal with just his third possession of the game.

The margin was 36 points at the main break. The Cats led the contested possession count 79-58. But the major talking point was Sam Reid, who limped to the bench just before the break. While the Cats had made the hard call on Max Holmes, Sydney had taken a risk, which had already backfired.

In the 2020 Grand Final, Geelong had led Richmond at the main break and let things slip. The players were well aware of that, but Scott was back preaching the same message. 'We have got two more quarters to get our game going as well as we can,' he said.

THIRD QUARTER

One minute into the second half Reid was substituted off with just four handballs to his name. Compounding that, back-to-back errors from the normally reliable Tom McCartin handed Geelong the opening two goals of the third quarter.

For the first he was run down by Duncan 15 metres out from goal and then his attempted short pass across goal was marked by Close. Any chance of a Swans comeback was shot as the Cats put the foot down, Smith kicking his third of the day off one step from 50 metres.

Cam Guthrie drew a free kick after Oliver Florent dived on the ball in the forward pocket for the next goal, before it officially became Stengle time. His fairytale year continued with two goals in three minutes, which suddenly had him in the Norm Smith Medal discussion.

The first came via a releasing handball to allow Stengle an easy around-the-body shot from 30 metres, while his fourth goal for the game came from a Dangerfield short pass that gave him what for most would be a tough shot from the boundary line – but not for the All-Australian forward pocket.

Dangerfield had owned the premiership quarter as the Cats piled on 6.3 to one point. The Cats' vice-captain had 10 disposals for the quarter, seven contested possessions, four score involvements, four inside-50s and three clearances. By contrast Sydney's resident superstar Buddy Franklin had been destroyed by Henry, with just three disposals and one mark.

As the players came into the huddle for the final time, the reality that they'd won the premiership was starting to sink in. The lead was now out to 74 points and they had another 30 minutes to enjoy the greatest day of their football careers.

Selwood was preparing himself for the final half-an-hour of his football life and he couldn't hide his emotions when he spoke to his teammates for the final time. He straightaway blurted out: 'We've won it.'

He then got back on message when he relayed something his first coach had instilled in him. Back in 2007 the Cats found themselves in a similar situation in the Grand Final against Port Adelaide. They were miles ahead at three-quarter time, but coach Mark Thompson had implored them to continue playing the game the right way, as that would be what would live in the memory bank.

As the coaches got in the lift to return to the box after three-quarter time, Scott still had his game face on. James Kelly gave him a gentle jab in the ribs and told the premiership coach he was allowed to smile now. 'We're going well mate,' Kelly said.

That got a smirk but Scott was determined to keep his emotions in check for at least another half-an-hour. But his favourite moment of the Grand Final was about to come, which would test his resolve.

FOURTH QUARTER

'I NEED to kick one mate.'

Jeremy Cameron knew who to ask. Dangerfield had been everywhere, and as they left the three-quarter time huddle he agreed to help his teammate out.

'Just run past me wherever it is on the ground,' Dangerfield said. He was a man of his word.

At the seven-minute mark Danger did what Danger had been doing all day. He got the clearance out of the centre square and then sprinted forward to get the return kick just inside the 50-metre arc. As he slowly walked back, Cameron started sprinting from the pocket and Dangerfield gave a quick handball – and his teammate swung around onto his trusted left boot to break his Grand Final goal drought.

It summed up the day for Sydney as much as anything. The Cats were playing with them and it was party time.

On the interchange bench Selwood found himself seated next to De Koning and Blicavs. The skipper's mind was beginning to wander, the heart was racing and the eyes were starting to water as he soaked up every moment of his farewell. His trance was broken up with three words from De Koning: 'You can't finish.'

Selwood was blown away that with everything that was going on the 21-year-old had read the moment. Blicavs could see his long-time teammate was in a bit of trouble, but for the kid to say that really moved the captain.

There were more tears of joy shortly after and this time they were up in the coaches' box.

Cam Guthrie had felt a twinge in his hamstring early in the final term. The football gods had done the right thing though, because the injury meant medical sub Brandan Parfitt would get to see some Grand Final action. He'd put on a brave face all week, even though he was hurting. When told he would be the sub, he vowed to the coaches: 'I will not let you down, I promise you. I will do whatever you need me to do.'

When Dangerfield marked deep out in the forward pocket, Parfitt headed towards the goal square. The set shot from the midfield superstar fell short, with Blicavs gathering it and shooting off a quick handball to Tuohy who tried to have a quick snap at goal. It didn't get through the Swans defenders but Close, who'd had some lovely deft touches throughout the afternoon, grabbed the ball and delivered the perfect no-look handball over his head to Parfitt, who quickly put boot to ball from 2 metres out.

The ecstasy on Parfitt's face as he did a fist pump in front of the Geelong fans was matched only by Scott's reaction in the coaches' box. He leapt to his feet, started screaming and banging the phone on the desk.

That was *the* moment of the Grand Final for the coach. All year the Cats had been about team first, and here was a player who'd deserved to be in the 22 but wasn't, yet he was getting the opportunity to be a part of this great day.

Five minutes later the coach was back up on his feet again when another unlikely goalkicker joined the party. Once again it had Dangerfield's fingerprints all over it. Despite being tackled by two Swans, his brute force allowed him to get a left-foot snap away, which was heading towards the goal, where De Koning was standing alone. The key defender had wandered down and gratefully marked the ball on his chest, kicking his first career goal from 1 metre out. That set off more pandemonium in the Geelong coaches' box while De Koning couldn't stop laughing as he jogged all the way back to full-back.

You'd think those two moments would be hard to top, but when it comes to Selwood fairytales do happen.

At the 24-minute mark Smith roved a boundary line throw-in and sent a wild handball towards the Cats 50-metre line, where Close jumped high and produced another delicate tap to Selwood, who took two steps and kicked the best goal of his 355-game career. He'd fashioned a banana on the run from 48 metres under extreme pressure. He watched it sail through as he lay on the ground and then put his hands to his face. The emotions were overflowing now. Dangerfield dragged him up as he continued to cover his eyes, as every Geelong player converged on their captain.

Joel Selwood kicks his last goal.

Immediately the Channel 7 commentators were speculating about whether the emotion was telling a story. The camera then panned to the stands, where his wife, Britt, and mother, Maree, weren't doing a great job of keeping the secret, as they were both in tears.

A minute later Cameron marked on the lead and as he was lining up to kick his second goal, Scott and his coaches arrived down on the interchange bench. There were more tears and lots of hugs as the final two minutes ticked away.

Max Holmes and the rest of the Cats' playing list had also made their way down onto the ground. Scott made sure one of his first hugs was for the Cats' heartbreak story.

Selwood took a mark on the outer wing, and the crowd on the Shane Warne Stand wing rose to their feet to applaud the greatest warrior in Geelong's history.

A late goal with 30 seconds to go from Papley was barely noticed as the celebrations were clicking into gear. All it meant was the final margin in the 2022 Grand Final was a stunning 81 points.

When the siren sounded all eyes went to Selwood. Close was the first to him and then the skipper went hunting for his best friend Hawkins. The big full-forward was a blubbering mess, tears streaming down his face as he hugged Selwood, refusing to let him go.

Cam Guthrie suddenly wasn't feeling his strained hamstring as he sprinted off the bench, first into the arms of his good mate Blicavs and then to his younger brother. Cameron and his partner in crime Close shared a special moment while the two Irishmen, Tuohy and O'Connor, did a jig together.

But the focus was on Selwood, the man who'd just led the oldest team in history to its 10th premiership. He was in the mind of Sydney co-captain Dane Rampe, who was the first behind the microphone for the official presentations. 'I just want to touch on Joel Selwood's record as well,' Rampe said. 'Sometimes you have got to pinch yourself when you share the field with giants of the game, and you are an absolute giant. Congratulations.'

The Geelong captain, who'd been one of his side's best with 26 disposals, eight marks and four tackles, was clearly moved as he addressed the sea of blue and white who were still dancing and singing in the stands.

'To my teammates, and the club, everyone involved in it – not just this year but the years gone by, I hope you're sitting back proud,' Selwood said. 'They are a hell of a group. To our 72,000-plus members, we can't thank you enough and jump back on board, these boys are so special. It's coming home, back where it belongs.'

Former Collingwood coach and captain Nathan Buckley had the honour of presenting the Norm Smith Medal. 'No relation,' he quipped when he announced Isaac Smith had won the honour.

Smith had an incredible stats sheet – 32 disposals, 14 score involvements, 11 inside-50s, five clearances, 12 marks, three goals and a game-high 771 metres gained. He'd received the maximum three votes from four of the five members of the voting panel to score 14 votes, four ahead of Dangerfield, boasting 27 disposals (19 contested), nine clearances, four tackles and 469 metres gained. Stengle received four votes for his four-goal haul, while young defender Sam De Koning got one vote, as did Blicavs.

The Selwood moments kept rolling when he gave the young Auskicker who'd presented him with his premiership medallion a pair of football boots. He then waited on stage for his coach to join him for the moment that few at the start of the season had thought possible.

Cameron Ling, who held the cup aloft in 2011 as captain, had been nominated by Geelong to hand over the premiership trophy – and he couldn't get it out of his hands quick enough. Scott and Selwood then gave their victory salute, raising the cup to the sky.

The rest of the Cats soon invaded the podium as blue and white confetti rained down on them. Eventually they dispersed for the slow lap of the MCG, where they found family and friends in the stands and took happy snaps with the premiership cup. Tuohy had the flag from his home town of Portlaoise around his neck, while Selwood dragged the Cats' water boy, Sam Moorfoot, out of the crowd.

He even used Sam's phone to ring his mum while still on the ground, telling her he was going to look after Sam and make sure he got back home safe to Geelong.

In a quiet moment Dangerfield stood still in the stadium, which was still buzzing, and took in what had just happened over the previous three hours.

'This is Everest. This is the pinnacle. This is what it means to be content,' he recalled. 'It was worth the wait and better than I could have ever imagined. I can't remember us playing a better game than the Grand Final in my time at Geelong. It was a complete game.'

CHAPTER 28

Aftermath

Joel Selwood pulled into the local APCO service station at Barwon Heads for some much-needed nourishment.

He had his pregnant wife, Britt, in the front seat and the 2022 Premiership Cup in the back seat. The clock had ticked past midnight after the biggest day of his long career. Seven hours earlier he'd won his first premiership as captain, his fourth premiership as a player – the first Cat to do so, which was the last in a long line of firsts – in what was his last game of football. He still hadn't said that publicly and had played a straight bat during a whirlwind couple of hours after the siren, which included multiple media interviews and lots of photos with family and friends.

There had been a mighty rendition of the Cats theme song, sung with much gusto on the last Saturday in September.

There had been a fans reception at Yarra Park, across the road from the MCG, before the bus finally got back down the highway, where the party kept rolling at GMHBA Stadium. Selwood was an experienced campaigner by now and knew not to go too hard on the Saturday night, given there were a few big days of celebration to come. Plus he wanted to get Britt home.

After he got his snacks Selwood got back in the car and suddenly realised something was missing ... the car key. Then it dawned on him. Harry Taylor had initially gone and got his car for him and obviously hadn't turned it off when they did a swap over into the driver's seat.

Selwood had driven home oblivious to the fact he didn't have the key, so now he was stranded. His house, where the spare key was, was a decent 10-minute walk away and the skipper and his wife were tired, so he improvised.

Dressed in a club tracksuit with his jumper still on, Selwood hailed down a young P-plater who had arrived at the service station. 'She had been working at the pub, her name was Emily and I asked if she could drop me home, so I jumped into her car,' Selwood said.

'I then asked her how her day was and she wasn't in the best of moods to be honest, as it was a busy day at the Barwon Heads pub. She didn't really pick up who I was at the time and then asked me how my day was and I said it was actually pretty good. Then she said what did I get up to and I said I actually played in the game today. She still hadn't picked up who I was, which was a nice thing, and then she asked for my name.

'When I said it she then started swearing at herself. We picked up the key and drove back to the car and I told Emily that I actually had the cup in the car and asked if she would like a photo. So she got a photo and drove back to Geelong.'

And yes – water boy Sam Moorfoot was home safe and sound too.

While Selwood was dealing with his own drama, the party had gone into the wee hours. Jeremy Cameron provided the highlight of the night when he got home to his farm just outside Geelong and put his premiership medallion on one of his cows, who walked off into the night. Thankfully he had it back by the time he arrived at the Family Day at Kardinia Park the following day. The key forward had been voted best on ground in the celebrations so far, but things went up a level at the traditional Mad Monday.

Geelong had a reputation for being the best in the business for their end-of-season party in regards to the time and effort they put into their costumes for the day. The great premiership team of 15 years ago had lifted the bar, with full-back Matthew Scarlett always one of the best dressed.

This year, with the media waiting outside the pub of club legend Billy Brownless near the waterfront, a retirement village bus pulled up out the front. First off was Patrick Dangerfield, complete with full make-up and grey hair spray, followed by Isaac Smith, who fell out of the bus as he struggled with his walking frame.

It was pure genius, a great riposte to the narrative that the Cats had been too old to win a premiership. The beers flowed freely on Monday, but on Tuesday morning Selwood had a job to do. He drove from Barwon Heads to his best mate Tom Hawkins' farm in nearby Ceres to tell him he was retiring.

While Hawkins and most of his close friends had suspected this might be the case, the euphoria of the victory and how well Selwood had played over the last month of the season had many thinking he might go around again.

There were more tears shed with Hawkins, who by his own admission is a very emotional unit, before Selwood made a stop at Mitch Duncan's house on the way home to reveal the news to him.

He had a quiet word to a couple of others, including Dangerfield, Mark Blicavs, Tom Stewart and Cam Guthrie, but he didn't want to take the attention away from the celebrations, which continued with a street parade on Tuesday. The players were required back at the club on Wednesday for exit meetings and memorabilia signing. That's when Selwood told the rest of his teammates.

'I was looking around the rooms and I just saw people that I wanted to go to work with and I'm wondering what I'm going to do next year and I'm not going to be with people like that,' he said. 'They've all been a joy. I just told them they're so lucky for being here and I've enjoyed their company. I'll turn into the biggest fan. I asked a couple of them if they'd find me some tickets because I've never had to do that before. I'm sure we'll work that out. Footy clubs are special. I'm in a really special one.'

He then faced the media to officially announce his retirement, his family and teammates cramming into the Captain's Room at GMHBA Stadium. There were several moments where he had to work hard to control his emotions, in particular when he was asked to rate the extraordinary achievements over 355 games and four premierships.

Selwood looked at Hawkins in the front row and started to tear up. 'It's the people you play with, it's the front row, it's not a stat,' he said. 'Hawk is a star, as I've played over

300 games with him which is ridiculous, but I can't put it [the greatest achievement] into a number thing for you. I just loved playing with the boys.'

Sitting next to him, Scott also couldn't help but get emotional for a player he described as the greatest he'd been associated with. 'When you take everything into consideration, he is the best player I've ever seen and the best representative of the Geelong footy club you could possibly imagine,' Scott said.

'We won the footy lottery getting to spend a decade or so with Joel Selwood and now it's the turn for others to see what a truly great person he is. You can forget about everything he has done on a footy field and the rest would still be amazing.'

List manager Andrew Mackie and recruiter Stephen Wells emerged out of the AFL's 10-day trade period acclaimed as its winners.

Two former Geelong Falcons returned home. First-round pick Tanner Bruhn was back after two years at the GWS Giants, while Ollie Henry, younger brother of premiership defender Jack, came back down the highway after two years at Collingwood. The Cats also brought in talented midfielder Jack Bowes in a complicated deal with the Gold Coast Suns.

Three weeks after Geelong had won the premiership by 81 points they were already getting stronger and better.

It was the Geelong way, as Cameron had learnt.

'We want to come back and get better,' he declared. 'That's something this list does. There are a lot of guys in their 30s but they look at different ways to get better each and every year, and next year it will be the same.'

Joel Selwood will be watching.

GEELONG'S 2022 SEASON SUMMARY

Club	Q1	Q2	Q3	Q4	Score	Margin	Result	Ground	Date	Ladder result
Round 1										
Geelong	7.5	12.9	17.14	20.18	138	66	WON	MCG	19 March	1
Essendon	2.1	3.3	6.3	11.6	72					
Round 2										
Sydney	4.3	11.3	15.4	17.5	107	30				
Geelong	2.4	6.7	8.13	10.17	77		LOST	SCG	25 March	7
Round 3										
Collingwood	3.7	4.11	13.12	13.13	91					
Geelong	2.3	6.4	9.6	16.8	104	13	WON	MCG	2 April	7
Round 4										
Geelong	2.2	7.6	9.8	11.14	80	10	WON	GMHBA	8 April	5
Brisbane Lions	2.2	6.3	10.3	11.4	70					
Round 5										
Hawthorn	5.3	8.4	10.4	14.8	92	12				
Geelong	1.4	6.6	11.10	11.14	80		LOST	MCG	18 April	7
Round 6										
North Melbourne	1.2	2.4	4.5	9.7	61					
Geelong	3.7	7.11	13.15	17.19	121	60	WON	Blundstone	24 April	6
Round 7										
Geelong	5.0	5.1	6.3	10.6	66		LOST	GMHBA	30 April	7
Fremantle	3.3	4.7	8.8	10.9	69	3				
Round 8										
GWS	2.2	3.5	3.9	4.11	35					
Geelong	4.3	6.7	8.11	12.16	88	53	WON	Manuka	7 May	5
Round 9										
St Kilda	2.2	4.4	11.8	13.12	90	10				
Geelong	4.3	6.8	8.10	11.14	80		LOST	Marvel	14 May	7
Round 10										
Geelong	3.6	4.8	9.11	11.16	82	35	WON	GMHBA	21 May	6
Port Adelaide	2.1	5.3	6.3	7.5	47					

Club	Q1	Q2	Q3	Q4	Score	Margin	Result	Ground	Date	Ladder result
Round 11										
Geelong	2.4	8.5	11.5	15.7	97	42	WON	GMHBA	28 May	6
Adelaide	0.6	3.7	6.11	7.13	55					
Round 12										
Western Bulldogs	1.5	4.6	6.9	10.10	70					
Geelong	7.2	8.6	8.8	12.11	83	13	WON	Marvel	3 June	4
Round 13 bye										
Geelong									14 June	5
Round 14										
West Coast	2.3	6.5	8.6	9.9	63					
Geelong	4.4	6.5	11.6	12.9	81	18	WON	Optus	18 June	4
Round 15										
Geelong	5.2	8.5	9.8	13.11	89	3	WON	MCG	25 June	2
Richmond	2.0	5.3	10.7	13.8	86					
Round 16										
Geelong	3.5	8.8	15.12	21.18	144	112	WON	GMHBA	2 July	2
North Melbourne	3.1	4.1	5.1	5.2	32					
Round 17										
Geelong	3.3	5.8	8.12	12.19	91	28	WON	GMHBA	7 July	1
Melbourne	3.1	5.4	7.6	9.9	63					
Round 18										
Carlton	4.1	5.1	6.3	8.7	55					
Geelong	3.4	7.6	10.8	12.13	85	30	WON	MCG	16 July	1
Round 19										
Port Adelaide	4.3	5.5	13.7	14.10	94					
Geelong	5.1	11.3	12.6	16.10	106	12	WON	Adelaide	23 July	1
Round 20										
Geelong	1.2	4.6	12.8	14.10	94	28	WON	GMHBA	30 July	1
Western Bulldogs	4.3	6.5	6.8	9.12	66					
Round 21										
Geelong	6.4	8.5	12.7	17.8	110	45	WON	GMHBA	6 August	1
St Kilda	3.0	7.1	7.4	10.5	65					

GEELONG'S 2022 SEASON SUMMARY

Club	Q1	Q2	Q3	Q4	Score	Margin	Result	Ground	Date	Ladder result
Round 22										
Gold Coast	2.2	4.2	7.2	9.5	59					
Geelong	7.3	12.5	15.9	18.11	119	60	WON	Metricon	13 August	1
Round 23										
Geelong	6.4	12.7	15.12	19.17	131	85	WON	GMHBA	20 August	1
West Coast	3.2	4.4	6.4	7.4	46					
First Qualifying Final										
Geelong	1.3	4.7	7.10	11.12	78	6	WON	MCG	3 September	
Collingwood	3.5	4.8	8.11	10.12	72					
First Preliminary Final										
Geelong	4.2	7.7	14.11	18.12	120	71	WON	MCG	16 September	
Brisbane Lions	2.0	3.1	5.2	7.7	49					
Grand Final										
Geelong	6.5	9.8	15.11	20.13	133	81	WON	MCG	24 September	
Sydney	1.0	4.2	4.3	8.4	52					

PLAYER STATISTICS

No.	Player	Games	Disposals	Marks	Handballs	Goals	Tackles	Inside 50	Clearances
30	Atkins, Tom	25	452	65	214	4	157	55	77
24	Bews, Jed	23	249	79	115	1	43	27	9
46	Blicavs, Mark	24	425	97	239	8	121	61	82
5	Cameron, Jeremy	24	388	141	116	65	34	75	14
15	Ceglar, Jonathon	3	35	2	19	-	2	4	15
45	Close, Brad	25	394	85	213	26	93	65	24
40	Dahlhaus, Luke	10	104	20	64	3	19	14	4
35	Dangerfield, Patrick	18	404	70	178	8	49	93	106
16	De Koning, Sam	23	281	120	138	1	6	15	1
28	Dempsey, Oliver	2	19	-	14	1	2	2	1
22	Duncan, Mitch	22	515	184	173	9	35	67	34
31	Evans, Francis	5	38	8	24	1	7	4	2
39	Guthrie, Cameron	25	613	90	297	12	124	73	108
29	Guthrie, Zach	21	321	116	97	5	48	47	4
26	Hawkins, Tom	25	328	142	107	67	39	42	24
38	Henry, Jack	17	184	82	65	4	24	14	2
4	Higgins, Shaun	5	83	15	42	1	19	11	9
9	Holmes, Max	18	280	68	119	13	42	52	24
10	Knevitt, Mitch	2	22	8	12	-	3	4	2
8	Kolodjashnij, Jake	23	276	107	111	2	33	19	7
27	Menegola, Sam	7	125	28	38	5	8	27	9
32	Miers, Gryan	22	327	80	153	13	47	57	8
19	Narkle, Quinton	8	68	21	28	4	8	14	9
33	Neale, Shannon	2	13	3	9	4	3	2	
42	O'Connor, Mark	22	277	84	106	56	37	11	
3	Parfitt, Brandan	17	348	32	180	5	80	59	74
17	Ratugolea, Esava	4	26	9	9	-	8	3	2
23	Rohan, Gary	12	108	31	37	14	29	33	4
14	Selwood, Joel	21	459	67	221	7	91	83	108
7	Smith, Isaac	24	517	161	178	15	31	123	18
1	Stanley, Rhys	20	256	64	111	3	36	56	65
18	Stengle, Tyson	25	361	82	114	53	64	86	34
12	Stephens, Cooper	7	76	14	40	-	11	12	14
44	Stewart, Tom	20	465	146	111	-	40	45	8
2	Tuohy, Zach	24	520	120	169	9	44	60	25

ACKNOWLEDGEMENTS

The publishers would like to thank the AFL, AFL Photos and the Geelong Football Club for their assistance. The author would like to acknowledge the news outlets, and football websites referenced during his research for this book, including the *Herald Sun*, *The Age*, afl.com.au, foxsports.com.au, Irish news outlet The42 and Geelong Football Club.